And Yet I Still Have Dreams

AND YET I STILL HAVE DREAMS

A Story of a Certain Loneliness

JOANNA WISZNIEWICZ

Translated from the Polish and with a foreword by Regina Grol

NORTHWESTERN UNIVERSITY PRESS
Evanston, Illinois

Northwestern University Press
Evanston, Illinois 60208-4170

English translation copyright © 2004 by Joanna Wiszniewicz and
Northwestern University Press. Published 2004. Originally published in Polish
in 1996 by Agencja Wydawnicza Tu, Warsaw, Poland, under the title *A jednak
czasem miewam sny. Historia pewnej samotności Joannie Wiszniewicz opowiedziana.*
Copyright © 1996 by Joanna Wiszniewicz.

Printed in the United States of America

10 9 8 7 6 5 4 3 2 1

ISBN 0-8101-1813-0 (cloth)
ISBN 0-8101-1814-9 (paper)

Library of Congress Cataloging-in-Publication Data

Wiszniewicz, Joanna.
[A jednak czasem miewam sny. English]
And yet I still have dreams : a story of a certain loneliness / Joanna Wiszniewicz ;
translated from the Polish and with a foreword by Regina Grol.
p. cm. — (Jewish lives)
ISBN 0-8101-1813-0 (cloth : alk. paper) — ISBN 0-8101-1814-9
(pbk. : alk. paper)
1. Wiszniewicz, Joanna. 2. Jews—Poland—Warsaw—Biography. 3. World
War, 1939–1945—Poland—Warsaw. 4. Warsaw (Poland)—Biography.
I. Title. II. Series.
DS135.P63W57813 2003
940.53'18'092—dc21
2003009754

The paper used in this publication meets the minimum requirements of the
American National Standard for Information Sciences—Permanence of Paper
for Printed Library Materials, ANSI Z39.48-1992.

Ms. Wiszniewicz completed the book within the framework of her research
program at the Jewish Historical Institute in Warsaw, Poland. The book was
published under the auspices of the Polish Ministry of Culture and National
Heritage. It received an honorable mention in the Culture Foundation (Poland)
literary competition.

✿

Contents

❉

Translator's Foreword

The Holocaust, an unprecedented event that challenged and under-
mined the fundamental premises of our civilization, continues
to hold a central, if problematic, place in humanity's collective consciousness. The staggering human toll of the Holocaust has been doc-
umented in numerous historical publications, memoirs, collections of
records and photographs, as well as scholarly works. Yet all too often
the Holocaust is either trivialized or coldly objectified and rendered in
language that transforms the victims into mere numbers. Facts and
figures, important as they are, do not reflect the full dimension of the
Holocaust, nor do the many memoirs that have flooded the publishing
market offering pain-filled yet stereotypical testimonials. That is why
the appearance of this book is so significant. Alex's "told narrative"
transcends the anonymity of mass slaughter and, more importantly,
subverts the stereotypes and shatters the templates of preconceived no-
tions about the Holocaust. It provides original and brutally honest
glimpses into one of the darkest periods of human history.

While—as some argue—the enormity of the horror endured by
victims of the Shoah may well exceed the expressive means of language, this book unveils the emotional, physical, and spiritual realities of the Holocaust in a most vivid manner. Although Alex, the
narrator of the book, entered the Warsaw ghetto at a very young age,
his account is that of an astute participant and a witness with a
tremendous capacity for recall who narrates the events with studied
detachment and without sentimentalizing. This is the primary reason
why *And Yet I Still Have Dreams* stands out among books on the Holocaust. Having spent his childhood on the "devil's playground," as Professor Piotr Wróbel refers to Poland during World War II, and having
faced death repeatedly, Alex survived the ghetto, as well as several

camps, forced marches, and labor in Germany. He recalls his experiences with critical distance, with optimal attempts at objectivity, and presents the grim material of ghetto and camp life in a new light— with an unsparing and unapologetic sharpness rarely found in Holocaust memoirs. In adult vocabulary and with great intellectual rigor, Alex reconstitutes his own emotions and observations as a child. His vantage point of an exceptionally intelligent adult is superimposed on that of an extremely sensitive and perceptive child, and this complex perspective yields rare, frank, and gripping insights into the perplexity and malignancy of the Holocaust.

One might say that this book offers a corrective vision of the Holocaust. Alex's language is dispassionate. He does not demonize the Nazis or aggrandize the Jews, nor does he consider the survivors, including himself, heroes for having survived. He dares to present the victims of the Holocaust, even his own family, in a less than flattering light. He is not afraid to express the admiration he and some other victims of the Holocaust, on occasion, had held for the Nazis. Nor does Alex shy away from accusing American Jewry of a herd instinct, an impulse to identify with the Holocaust and a surfeit of artificial ancestral memory. Alex totally rejects, moreover, competitive victimology or martyrdom. In contrast to the oft-repeated slogan "Never forget!" (*Zkor!*; literally, remember), he advocates putting the Holocaust behind us and no longer utilizing it as a rallying cry of American Jewry. Few survivors of the Holocaust share his views or would risk voicing them with such candor.

And Yet I Still Have Dreams offers more than insights and lessons about the Holocaust. In addition to discussing his rich cultural life in the ghettos and camps (despite the Nazi terror), the narrator also presents us with illuminating remarks about representatives of the secular Jewish intelligentsia in the pre-World War II period and the gradual and complex process of their assimilation into Polish society. He recognizes their tangled sense of identity, which entailed, as in the case of Alex's mother, a formal identification with Jewishness along with its emotional rejection. His father's and other relatives' processes of identity formation are diverse yet equally complex and fascinating. So is Alex's own route. His unique biography and his family's particular history have set him further apart from Jewish traditions and conventional paths toward developing a sense of self.

As a grandson of a Jew who became a Polish senator, Alex intro-
duces the reader to an elite cultural milieu rarely presented in literature of the Holocaust. Equally revelatory are his comments about his
own adaptation to life in the United States after World War II, his
own process of forging his identity or, to be more precise, his constant
effort to avoid the "snares of Jewish identity." Likewise, Alex's comments about the contrasts between Polish and American Jewry are
most noteworthy.

The exceptional merit of this book results also from the serendipi-
tous conjuncture of a very capable interviewer meeting a very intelligent and responsive interviewee. The penetrating questions posed to
Alex by Joanna Wiszniewicz, the "absentee interviewer" of this vol-
ume, contribute to its quality. While her questions have been excised
from the published text, one can infer them from the narrative struc-
ture. Ms. Wiszniewicz is a hidden interlocutor in the book, allowing
Alex to hold center stage and to be constantly in the foreground. Yet,
while standing in the wings, she engages the narrator in a fascinating
dialogue and elicits information that could have easily been glossed
over or totally ignored. Given the coherence and poignancy of the vol-
ume, she also deserves credit for transforming a nine-hundred-page
record of interviews into a condensed, eminently readable, and gripping narrative that preserves the narrator's style.

That style—choppy, colloquial, direct, yet often interspersed with
sophisticated terminology—constituted a challenge in rendering the
book into English. While my objective as a translator has always been
to stay as close as possible to the spirit, the letter, and the style of the
original text, in the case of this book I had to make certain concessions
for the sake of clarity. I felt compelled, on a number of occasions, to
transform sentence fragments of the Polish version into complete sen-
tences in English or to interfere in matters of paragraphing. For the
most part, however, the choppy quality of Alex's narration is preserved. Another considered intrusion on my part was tampering with
tenses. The sequence of tenses (*consecutio temporum*), which is called for
in English, is not required and, thus, often totally ignored in Polish.
In the original, Alex fluctuates between the present and the past tense,
favoring the former. Present-tense narration has a more powerful impact and often produces a greater sense of immediacy. Though mind-
ful of that, I have been forced to change Alex's story into past tense to

avoid the fluctuations in his account and to eliminate the potential for confusion about the timing and sequence of events. Where I have chosen not to intrude is in the matter of names. I have preserved the Polish spelling of names (with the exception of the name Mania, which I have changed to Manya) even when English equivalents exist or diminutive forms of first names were used in the original.

To preserve the authentic flavor of the original, I have retained a few foreign terms and have used them without explanation in an attempt to minimize as much as possible intrusions that might distract the reader from the riveting narrative. Perhaps the most unfamiliar terms—particularly to young readers or novices in the realm of literature of the Holocaust—are the Polish term *szmalcownik* (pronounced "shmaltsovnik"; a double-crossing profiteer); the Latin term *numerus clausus* ("a closed number" or quota, referring to a restricted and very small number of Jews accepted to Polish universities); and the German terms *Aktion* and its plural *Aktionen* (meaning capturing and execution of Jews) or *Judenrat* (the Jewish Council, an institution established by the Nazis and made responsible for all essential affairs in the ghetto: the distribution of food, allocation of apartments, work, public services, collection of taxes, and so forth).

The English version of the book is inevitably the product of three voices and three sensibilities—Alex's, Joanna Wiszniewicz's, and mine. I hope to have succeeded as a translator in being as unobtrusive as possible, in giving precedence to Alex's voice, and having avoided any loss of meaning in his profoundly penetrating and illuminating narrative.

The publication of this book is very timely. The generation of eyewitnesses is dying off. The clock is running out on history. As Eli Zborowski, chairman of the American Society for Yad Vashem, aptly put it,

> Quite literally, when it comes to eyewitness testimony about the Holocaust, you and I are living in history's eleventh hour. The last of those who survived the horrors of the Nazi regime are now succumbing to time.
>
> Right now we must confront the very real possibility that within a generation—or less—there will be no one left who saw the Shoah firsthand . . .

. . . no grandparents to impart their stories to grandchildren . . .

. . . no survivors to speak at schools, colleges, or civic organizations . . .

. . . and above all, no witnesses left to testify about mankind's darkest hour.

Alex's testimony not only individualizes the Holocaust and recaptures the climate of horror, providing an indelible sense of the realities of the Shoah. It also sheds light on Jewish life both before and after World War II and, in more general terms, on the formation of a sense of self by individuals subjected to persecution and cultural transplantation. His knowledge is not merely experiential or intuitive; it is also the result of extensive reflection, introspection, and erudition acquired over many years. Even the subtitle of this book—"A Story of a Certain Loneliness"—points to Alex's exploration of an important yet common human predicament. In his treatment of loneliness, the topic acquires very broad dimensions—personal, generational, ethnic, and metaphysical.

This is truly an exceptional book. Alex's insights will enlighten the reader in a myriad of ways. Above all, his comments on human nature and conduct in extreme situations may bring us much closer to grasping the "unimaginable," the moral incomprehensibility of the Holocaust.

Regina Grol
Professor of Comparative Literature
Empire State College
State University of New York

Acknowledgments

The translator acknowledges with gratitude Professors Ann Colley, Rosemary Feal, Claire Kahane, Carolyn Korsmeyer, and Emily Tall, as well as John Phelan, Esq., who have read and commented on all or significant portions of the translation. For technical assistance with the manuscript, special thanks go to Sheree Martinelli and John Farrell.

✤

Author's Introduction

It is difficult to write about matters that are finished, completed, such as my unusual experience with this book. It began innocently—an American Jew, a retired computer analyst born in Warsaw before World War II, was planning a trip to Poland. As a person residing in Poland, I was asked to take him under my wing. I met him, we started talking, and just a few days later I already knew that our conversation would be among the most significant in my life. Alex opened before me the most important world—the Jewish world of my parents' generation. To us, children of Holocaust survivors born in Poland after the war, essentially, this world was never revealed. In a peculiar way, it was enveloped in silence, lied about, negated.

By 1992, when Alex came to Poland, we—the first post–World War II generation of Polish Jews—knew very well that there were lacunae in our knowledge of our own roots, and we were quite advanced in making up for our lifelong arrears. During the 1980s, the last decade of crumbling Communism, some of us had begun to steep ourselves in the mysteries of Jewish religion and tradition. And yet for me and many of my peers the search for traces of our Jewishness in religion and tradition was not sufficient. It seemed to miss the point; it didn't advance us toward the understanding of our authentic roots. After all, these roots were nearby, very close to us, in the life of the generation immediately preceding ours. Ostensibly, they were within our reach! Yet, in 1992, they appeared more enigmatic to us, more difficult to uncover, than the exotic knowledge we were gaining about our ancestors' timeless Jewish tradition.

Overcoming the silence of one's parents is never easy, even when the silence is not that of an individual but of an entire generation. That is why all of us had to look for ways of understanding our parents' generation on our own, and each of us found his or her own milestones along the way. For me the conversation with Alex was such a milestone, one that unveiled my own Jewish tradition—the tradition of not cultivating Jewishness but rather departing from it, with all the concomitant psychological and cultural consequences.

With his phenomenal psychological perceptiveness, his unswerving pursuit of truth, and his uncanny sense of hearing, which made him detect even the slightest false note in anyone's behavior or conversation, Alex was an exceptional guide into that tradition. There were no questions he would not answer nor any "sacred cows" he would not look at closely to reexamine them. Alex's single-mindedness in unveiling the truth prompted me to venture into a territory I had previously tried very much to avoid—unexpectedly we started talking about the Holocaust. (Hence subsequently this book.) And here, too, Alex revealed to me something new, not because of what he told me (after all, individuals of my generation raised in Poland knew a great deal about the Holocaust) but because of how he talked about it. In his accounts the Holocaust was demythologized to the point of pain.

My conversations with Alex, which lasted several weeks, could not have happened at a different time or in a different place. They occurred at a perfect juncture when two people met and one was very eager to listen while the other had the desire to tell. At that time, I was open and receptive to any questions regarding Jewishness, and, as it seems to me now, looking for answers to them constituted for Alex more than merely an intellectual challenge. Such a moment, however, a moment of intimate understanding related to one theme, cannot last very long. For me as well as for Alex, it is now a matter of the past. We have remained good friends, but we cannot discuss Jewish topics any more. I no longer ask nor listen (because I have found many answers to the questions that preoccupied me), and he, with his spirit of contrariety, doesn't want to talk about it at all. "It's become 'the Shoah business!' Let's leave it alone," he often says with annoyance. Frankly, I sometimes wonder whether I should not concede that there may be a kernel of truth in his opinion.

Alex is not very happy that this book is being published in English. I had trouble getting him to authorize the earlier Polish edition as well. "That's not my voice," he grumbled upon his first reading. I had to record six more tapes of interviews with him and to write a large portion of the book anew before he finally—and reluctantly—authorized its publication (yet, without permission to reveal his last name).

Now he has an additional reason for discontent: "People will recognize me in your book even though you are not using my name. Now that it will be published in English, everybody will take me for some kind of a Holocaust-hysteric! You have to write in your introduction that the narrator has nothing to do with me!"

I don't know how much my narrator has in common with Alex. I suppose as much as he told me about himself and as much as my imagination created out of his story. The Alex of my book is a "creation," of course. He is my "creation" spawned in a condensed text based on a nine-hundred-page transcript of our interviews. He is also a "creation" (or "self-creation") of Alex himself, who presented himself to me, the eager interviewer, the way he wanted to present himself.

So, is this text truthful? The question belongs to the domain of phenomenology rather than to that of historical documentation. The text is truthful to the extent that Alex's factual and social memory, as well as his psychological intuition, are accurate. It is not truthful to the extent that *my* intuition and imagination, which I applied to the text in order to connect the interrupted threads of conversation and to impose a chronological order and dynamic, failed me.

I wrote this book under the impact of Alex's uncompromising endeavor to formulate the truth. And while writing, I, too, made every effort to reach that objective. That is why I accepted with humility Alex's snide remarks; I recorded additional interviews; I introduced corrections. I was grateful to him because I knew that if any false note sounded in the book, he would immediately point it out to me.

Initially, my intended audience was the generation of my peers, that is, children of Jewish Holocaust survivors residing in Poland. When the book was published in Poland, however, it turned out that the pre-World War II generation also found resonance with it; that Poles read the book as well; and that various fragments inspired various readers in a variety of ways. That is why, despite Alex's reluctance, I have decided to make the book available to the English-language reader.

Will the reader's different historical and cultural background make the reading of the book more difficult or easier? To what extent will the message of the book prove to be truly universal? To what extent is it local? If Alex is right about the growing "Shoah business" in the United States, will that context take away from the book's air of authenticity?

Such are the questions I pose to myself these days with some apprehension.

Joanna Wiszniewicz

And Yet I Still Have Dreams

ALEX'S NARRATIVE

✿

I

Once, when I was walking down the street with my mother—this was before the war, I must have been eleven—I noticed a man who attracted my attention. He had expressive Mediterranean eyes and curly hair. "What a good looking man! How handsome!" I said to my mother, expressing my admiration. "Handsome? He's not handsome at all. He has got such a Jewish face!"

That remark struck me, because he looked very much like my father.

My parents fell in love during World War I, before either of them enrolled at the university. The Russians wanted to draft my father (Warsaw was in the section of Poland under Russian rule before World War I), so he hid in my mother's parents' house on Tłomackie Street. These two Warsaw families had known each other for generations, and that's how it all began.

My mother's grandfather, my great-grandfather, was—as my family used to put it—"renowned for his piety." Allegedly, he built synagogues. He was a Jewish patriarch, a very Orthodox Jew. He raised his son, my mother's father (that is, my grandfather), in a firmly religious spirit, letting him read only religious texts in Hebrew. Nothing secular or in Polish was allowed. But my grandfather secretly read all the forbidden books. He taught himself Polish; he educated himself.

Grandfather was typical of the transitional period. He belonged to a generation that was still deeply rooted in the traditional model of Jewish life, but his own life was already leaning toward the West, toward the secular. He prayed as every pious Jew should, but he sent his children to secular schools and spoke only Polish to them. Though he was an important figure in the Agudat Israel Party, an orthodox Jewish party averse to assimilation, he wore normal European clothes and had a short beard. Realizing that Jewish tradition would not be passed on to me by my fully assimilated parents, Grandfather paid for my private Hebrew lessons, and yet he talked to me more often about politics than about God. He observed the Sabbath and all Jewish holidays scrupulously but performed the ritual part largely himself, allowing family gatherings to take on a mainly intellectual character.

I adored holidays and Sabbaths spent at Grandfather's on Tłomackie Street. Lit candles, wine on the table, togetherness. And above all, conversation. Sometimes my parents wanted me to stay home, either because it was late or for some other reason, but I would throw temper tantrums until they took me along. I always wanted to be there and to know what they talked about.

Mostly, they spoke about the threat of war and anti-Semitism, about how the situation of the Jews was becoming unbearable. My family would then split into two camps: one favorable to the Poles, the other hostile to them. "The Poles hate us, they're anti-Semitic by nature," said some uncles. "The Poles are remarkably tolerant and peaceful not to be knifing the Jews given the virulent anti-Semitic propaganda!" said others, including my grandfather.

Hearing all this must have made me pretty confused. Aunt Manya, father's sister, whom I considered an authority, said the Poles were pretty narrow-minded, provincial, unimaginative, and conceited. Father's second sister, Aunt Dora, on the other hand, saw a hundred thousand shortcomings in the Jews and ridiculed their expressive way of talking and gesturing.

My mother played yet another role. She was too intelligent and too refined to talk about Jews with the contempt that Aunt Dora displayed, but she took a similar view of things. For instance, when she constantly chided me for excessive gesticulation or bad manners, I sensed that she was really saying: "Don't behave like a Jew; don't talk loudly like a Jew." And she was also of the—probably subconscious—opinion that a man with Semitic features could not be considered handsome. In a way, Mother had interiorized anti-Semitic standards of beauty, anti-Semitic stereotypes. She must have done it unconsciously, and I am convinced that had I tried to talk to her openly about it, she would have denied everything indignantly. But her whole being expressed this inner contradiction: a formal identification with Jewishness and its emotional rejection.

Of course, I picked up all these clues on a more or less conscious level. Over time, they began to accumulate inside of me and transformed into that old Jewish disease: dislike of oneself.

I don't know which way my mother would have gone had she married someone other than my father. He was completely free of her complexes and ethnic prejudices. He was who he was and he had no problems with his identity. He read both Polish and Yiddish newspapers, knew both Polish and Yiddish literature. I don't think my mother could read Yiddish at all. I remember that, when my parents occasionally spoke about literature, over dinner, with my Hebrew teacher, Hesio Fenster, Father always mentioned Jewish writers with admiration and quoted Yiddish novels, extracting from them their specific ethnic flavor, while Mother kept going on about Prus and Żeromski, always displaying a clear preference for mainstream Polish literature with its portrayal of upper-class life.

My father's father, that is, my second grandfather, was also, like my mother's father, a religious Jew. He prayed; he went to the synagogue, but—like my other grandfather—sent his children to secular schools, and Polish ones to boot. My father, for example, graduated from the Górski High School.

What's interesting, my father, with his Polish education, aspired less to Polishness than did my mother, who had graduated from a Jewish school. It was she, not my father, who felt oppressed by her Jewish heritage. Later, already as an adult, I often wondered what one's identity truly depends on.

My father attended the synagogue only during the important holidays—Yom Kippur, Rosh Hashanah. He took me along. We wore yarmulkes. Father used to put on the tallith, but he behaved unlike the others. He didn't rock back and forth and didn't recite the prayers aloud. He read them as you would read a book. For him participating in Jewish holiday services was simply a symbol of belonging.

And for me? I couldn't even read Jewish prayers. I was simply bored.

Poles practically never visited us at home, though father knew a lot of them. As a financial director of the Jewish Hospital in the Czyste neighborhood (today it's the Wolski Hospital), he had frequent business contacts with them. He didn't *not* invite them home because of any antipathy on his part. On the contrary, father was very open-minded. Yet maintaining relations with Poles would have been unnatural for us. It would have looked as if we were having Poles over only because they were Poles. And an invited Pole might not have wanted that, might have felt uncomfortable with us.

Whether they intended it or not, my parents' attitude rubbed off on me. I remember being on a train to the seaside one summer. There was a Polish family with a boy my age in our compartment. The two of us had great fun during the whole trip and we exchanged addresses. The following day I told my parents I was going to visit my new Polish friend. "No, you can't," my mother said. "Why not?" I asked. "Because," she answered. I pestered her until she told me that his parents might not like it because I was a Jew.

In time I myself began to see things that way. In 1937, when I was ten, my secular Jewish school organized a trip to Vilna (it was a Polish city then). We slept on bunk beds in a large room at a youth hostel. Once, when I was putting my shoes on, I sat for a moment on the lower bunk, which was assigned to some girl from another school, a Polish one, and she began scolding me terribly. I immediately thought that it was because I was Jewish. She might have done it for some other reason—that I was a boy, for instance, or that sitting on her bed sheets with my clothes on was not hygienic—but the only explanation that occurred to me was that she didn't want a Jew touching her bed.

People usually think that Jews didn't socialize with Poles because of anti-Semitism, because of the Poles' reluctance. That's a great oversimplification. Anti-Semitism in the 1930s was terrible, to be sure. I remember my uncles telling me about the classroom ghettos, and the days when my mother wouldn't let me go out because there were anti-Semitic gangs roaming the streets. However, anti-Semitism alone cannot account for the barrier between Poles and Jews in those years. Had my parents wanted to establish social ties with the Poles, it would have involved a great deal of effort on their part to bridge the cultural gap. It would have been like me wanting to make friends with blacks in

America, where I have lived for the past forty years. Am I a racist? No.
Am I prejudiced against blacks? Absolutely not. But do I have black
friends? No. Why? Who knows?

I don't think that the isolation of an ethnic group in any country is
exclusively the result of conscious rejection. There are kinds of behavior that draw some people together while alienating others. Even during my childhood there were Jews who were more assimilated than
others, whose ties with Poles were stronger. There were families who
had become assimilated as early as the nineteenth century—all those
great Mendelson, Kacenelson, or Szenicer families. Or take writers
such as Wat or Leśmian. They must have had many Polish friends. And
yet, if you look at it more closely, the women Leśmian fell in love with
were all Jewish!

I have just read the memoir of a Pole. There wasn't a word about
Jews in it! He didn't know them at all. All he has is a childhood memory that when his family was forced to sell its estate, after the defeat of
the Poles' January 1863 uprising against the Russians, some Morde-
chaj was crying. Indeed, the two nationalities lived somewhat apart
from each other.

It was always obvious to me that the Poles were different, that they
lived differently. They interested me and appealed to me, but their
way of life and their behavior were somewhat alien to me. Their into-
nation was flatter, less emotional than ours (I always recognized them
by the way they talked). They weren't as direct and straightforward as
we were but more restrained, reserved. Their wit was dry and cool.
They were elegant and formal.

I remember an event that made me aware of these differences. One
summer, my parents and their friend, Mr. Rozen, were playing bridge
with a Polish family in the resort town of Inowłódz. (The two families
met because the owner of the boarding house was a liberal Polish lady
who advertised her vacancies in both the Polish and the Jewish press.)
One night the Polish couple's son came into the room where they were
playing and asked his father something in a very roundabout and dis-
creet way. It was obvious that he needed to have a pee but didn't want
to say so explicitly. His father felt embarrassed and was whispering
something to the boy, when Mr. Rozen, who had realized instantly
what was going on (the witty, intelligent Mr. Rozen whose features
and prominent nose combined to give him the look of a hundred Jews

put together), boomed: "Well, there's nothing to be ashamed of! You could have just said what you meant!" Then he pronounced the word with tactless relish.

I was a child at the time, but I sensed the confrontation of the Polish and the Jewish mentalities very clearly. The Poles must have thought: "That Rozen fellow is a typical Jew: crude, vulgar, uncouth, and forward." While Rozen was probably thinking: "That Pole with his priggish manners! What a hypocrite! I'll teach him a lesson!"

When I was little, I used to talk to God whenever I felt sad and alone. Sometimes I made up songs for him. My parents often went to the theater in the evening or to visit friends and left me alone with the maid. I went to bed feeling miserable and complained to God. I wanted him to console me. I cried. God was old, good, stern, and had a beard. Sometimes I asked my grandfather from Tłomackie Street, my mother's father, whether God knew what I was doing. "Yes, he knows what you are doing and he's watching over you," Grandfather answered. Now I realize that he was saying it as if he didn't really want to convince me, as if he knew that the God of his father would no longer be my God.

Sometimes I ask myself what my maternal grandfather's relations with God were like. I can't always find an answer to that question. I think that Grandfather's faith was simply something he was born into. I don't think he gave the matter much thought. Nowadays people have a choice. They can believe in God or not; they can chose this religion or that. When my grandfather was born, however, one believed because one's forefathers believed. One believed in the God of one's ancestors. That's all there was to it.

My grandfather from Tłomackie Street considered himself a religious Jew, but he applied his energy to secular matters. He was an ambitious politician, one of the leaders of the Agudat Israel Party, then a Jewish senator in the Polish parliament, and also a town councilor. Deep down, he probably expected that a secular, modern, and tightly knit Jewish community would emerge in Poland, and he wanted his children to be prepared for it. He must have assumed that this future secularized Jewish people would have friendly relations with the Poles (whom he respected greatly), though he certainly would not have wanted Jews to fully blend in with the Polish society.

Grandfather felt attached to Jewish tradition. I suppose it must have hurt him to see how reluctantly I learned Hebrew, how I was barely able to utter syllables in the language sacred to him. I feel that he accepted my secularization as the price of modernity. He also seemed to accept my parents' position, a position outside of both the Jewish tradition and the Polish community.

Was my grandfather fully aware of the contradictions inherent in his way of thinking? I doubt it. A person can have many contradictory desires, especially if he happens to live in a period of such profound changes. Yet I am sure that while his prayers were heartfelt and honest, he also had honest intentions to pave a road to modernity for his children. Sometimes things that seem illogical on the surface are coherent and make perfect sense from the psychological point of view.

My parents never talked about God with me. They never claimed God existed, nor that he didn't. They put it this way: "It's a complex problem that you are too young to understand. When you grow up, you'll be able to draw your own conclusions." For them religion was each person's private business; religious views were something to be respected and not tampered with.

My parents were liberal democrats who believed in tolerance, freedom of speech, a parliamentary system, separation of church and state. They believed that every human being had the same worth regardless of the person's social standing. Mother always taught me to raise my cap to my elders, even when they were simple people. I liked that.

None of the political parties in prewar Poland, in my view, were capable of representing my parents' political interests. They were not nationalists, neither Polish nor Jewish. They were not Communists because they were put off by the antidemocratic character of Communism. They were not Socialists because they believed in the free market economy. Above all, they were not Poles. Even my mother would not have called herself a Pole. A Polish Jew, yes, but not a Pole, despite the fact that she spoke and read only Polish and that she knew Polish literature so well. These paradoxes were typical not only of my mother, but my parents' circle—the liberal, assimilated Jewish intelligentsia— as a whole. It was an entire community, a community of neither Poles nor Jews, but of assimilated Jews! I remember them well, those Jewish lawyers, doctors, professors, mathematicians. They were secular, educated, spoke only in Polish, and kept together.

What did they have in common? All of them were breaking away from the Jewish religious tradition and moving toward modernity. It was an exceptionally traumatic journey. The shift to modernity is difficult for any nation, but it was particularly traumatic for the Jews. The traditional Jewish community didn't even contain the seeds of modernity! It was stuck in the Middle Ages. It had a very rich religious culture, but it did not have a secular culture—secular philosophy, sociology, or journalism (what did exist were secondary phenomena borrowed from European cultures and introduced into the Yiddish language). It did have a literature, but an intelligent person cannot confine his reading to a few novels. Jews opting for secularization had to abandon their rich culture. They had to reach for foreign cultures and foreign languages and enter modernity through them. Other nations did not lose their culture in making the transition to modernity. Jews had to renounce everything.

What was left for Polish Jews after that renunciation? An empty space, a space without roots. Polish culture, though secular, was too strongly infused with Catholic elements for Jews to fully assimilate into it. It was too distant, too alien for them. They spoke Polish, read Polish books, adopted the culture intellectually but could not fully do so emotionally. That's the way they remained—suspended between what they had left behind and what they could never attain. Culture, after all, is something more than a language and a literature. It's also a way of life rooted in religion and customs. Our forefathers do have some power over us. Changing a culture is never a simple matter. Sometimes I think that the painful journey my parents' generation had embarked upon resembled the wanderings of Jews led by Moses out of Egypt. They marched through Sinai for forty years and many died without reaching the destination. My parents' generation also had a long way to go. And they, too, had their sacrifices.

My father was able to go through all of it unharmed. He kept a clear sense of identity; he knew who he was and was free of complexes. Not so my mother, for all her interiorized anti-Semitic prejudices, her pro-Polish snobbery and her simultaneous avoidance of contacts with Poles. . . . Today I think that there might have been a kind of shallowness to her life, despite her great intelligence, her intellectual acumen, her college degree in French. . . . She had lost something along the way. She had no roots; she didn't belong to any tradition.

Could she have avoided this lack of rootedness? No. Because it was my grandfather who had started cutting off the roots. He was the one who sent her to a secular school, who spoke Polish with her, who modified the Sabbath customs so that they were no longer a continuation of the Jewish tradition but became simply our family's tradition. My grandfather led my mother out into Sinai. She had to make the rest of the journey from one culture to another on her own.

Others from her generation trod the same path, equally torn, equally devoid of roots, tradition, and identity. They walked for a long time. Even if some of them did reach their destination, the hardships of the journey left a mark on them—the mark of uncertain identity. Partially, I have inherited that mark as well.

❉

2

In 1933, my parents sent me to school. It was a modern private school for children of the assimilating Jewish middle class. What was Jewish about the school? Just the fact that only Jewish children went there. Maybe these facts, too: Once a week, we were taught Jewish history; there was no Catholic priest in the school, and we were not taught Catholic religion.

We read patriotic Polish literature in class. During school assemblies we recited patriotic Polish poems. We sang with ardor the song of Piłsudski's freedom fighters, "We, the First Brigade."*

Who did we identify with, singing the "we"? In whose name were we singing this "we"? Who were these "we" to us?

I don't know. But these are good questions.

I was very surprised when one day an uncle said to me: "You, too, will be a grown-up some day. You are three years old now, but some day you'll be a grown-up." I didn't expect that it could happen like this. My world of a three-year-old was divided into grown-ups and children. Actually, this was the only division of the world I knew at that time.

When later I discovered yet another division into Jews and non-Jews, that also surprised me. But I was most surprised when I found out (at the age of eight) that I, as a Jew, was not allowed to do things. "When I grow up, I'll enroll in a military academy and become an

---

* Song of the Polish legions fighting for Poland's independence under the command of Józef Piłsudski (1867–1935) during World War I. Piłsudski, creator of the legions and later Marshall of the free Poland, was beloved by his soldiers and became a symbol of Polish patriotism and an object of general veneration.

officer," I declared on some occasion to my grandfather, the senator. "You can't. They accept only Poles."

"What if . . . I were to convert to Catholicism?" Grandpa lifted up his cane and started hitting me.

I understood why he reacted that way only after several days of explanations. First my mother, then my uncle, then again my mother explained to me over and over again: You don't have to be religious, you don't have to go to the synagogue, you don't even have to observe the Sabbath. But *to convert?* To change one's identity?! That is ignoble. That is denial of one's self. That is denial of one's ancestors.

The dream of becoming a Polish officer never died in me. But I realized that it would never come true. The contempt with which my entire family responded to my idea of conversion and total polonization stopped me in my tracks. I understood that conversion meant total loss of any connection with the Jews and that it involved some kind of betrayal, some kind of absolute disloyalty.

I remained a Polish patriot for almost two more years. The public life in Poland had such a nationalistic tone, a soldier was a hero. . . . On the radio, legionnaires' songs were being played constantly; teachers from my Jewish school took us to the National Museum to admire the painter Matejko. . . .

I knew by heart Sienkiewicz's "Trilogy," a birthday gift from my mother. I subscribed to *The Flame* and *The Little Flame,* Polish children's magazines instilling patriotism. At least once a week, I looked at paintings of Polish landscapes—by Chełmoński, Wyczółkowski, Fałat—which were in my senator grandfather's apartment on Tłomackie Street. I devoured stories about King Boleslav Chrobry (the Bold), about the battle of Grunwald; I immersed myself in the reading of the novel *The Loyal River;* I was passionately interested in Polish uprisings, in the year 1920.*

I already knew that as a Jew I would never be accepted into the Polish officers' school because of the *numerus clausus.*

I knew I would have difficulties getting into a good state-owned Polish high school or certain departments at the university. I knew

---

* In the above paragraphs the narrator refers to literary works, paintings, songs, and historical events that belong to the canon of Polish patriotic education.

that there was anti-Semitism in Poland, but I was totally wrapped up in the Piłsudski mythology.

I was a Polish patriot.

This patriotism of mine was subjected to difficult tests. The toughest one was my father's laughter. Each time he heard me speak about Poland in this journalistic-patriotic manner, with me using the characteristic nationalist "we," he would mock me instantly: "Well, well, well, we, we, we, our Polish mountains, our Polish rivers. Do you think this is national consciousness? This is herd consciousness! The consciousness of a herd! Our Polish fields, our Polish forests, our 'we' . . ."

He ridiculed all of it. And I knew that he was not attacking Poland. He was attacking extremist nationalism, excessive phraseology, mindless anti-individualism. Had I presented the Zionist ideology to him in an equally emotional manner, he would have reacted the same way. "Be a master of your own mind! Don't let anyone brainwash you!" My father questioned identification with *any* kind of "we."

Another person undermining my attraction to collective sentiments was my classmate, Stefan Wandel. He came from a family with Communist leanings and ardently expressed Communist views. "Culture is a lie," he attempted to convince me. "Patriotism, national loyalty—it doesn't matter whether it's Polish, Jewish, or any other—amount to a false bourgeois consciousness!" His arguments weren't entirely clear to me, but the spirit of rebellion in Stefan's murky Communism, his urge to negate all values, appealed to me.

Today I know that I like to be independent, antiauthoritarian, and even when I do make an attempt to become a part of a collective, all at once a kind of compulsive giggle takes hold of me, a tickling, uncontrollable, self-mocking laughter. Do I attribute it to the influence of my "antiherd" father and Stefan Wandel, who negated everything? Or was I just born like that?

I remember that the "herd" has always been something that both attracted and repelled me. When Stefan Wandel suggested we form a small "clique" to oppose the group that had formed around Michał Chazan, our brutal class bully, I was delighted, delighted to break out of the mass! To be in a small group, conscious of its size and proud of it! But two years later, when the Jewish Scout organization was established in our school (actually, Jewish groups constituted part of the Polish Scouts), my attitude toward "herding" turned out to be totally different. I joined the "herd," went to meetings, played the games, saluted. I participated with enthusiasm in this cultivation of collective solidarity, discipline, and anti-individualism. It turned out that I liked it! Despite the occasional thought that my saluting was ridiculous, I accepted it!

I enjoyed being in the "herd." Could it be that being in a herd is always enjoyable?

This kind of an inner split, a conflict between my emotions and my consciousness is a constant motif of my life. It appears in various situations. I know that something is ridiculous, yet I do it. I know that some dream of mine doesn't make sense, and yet I dream it. I know that some anxiety is absurd, yet I can't get rid of it.

Such lack of integration is a common Jewish affliction. Of course, you don't have to be Jewish to have a split personality. Also, you can be a Jew with a very integrated mind, like my father. But the problem with the Jewish disintegration is similar to the problem with TB; you live in poor conditions, eat poorly, and yet don't get sick. But if you have a predisposition to TB . . .

If you are Jewish, grow up in an assimilating family, your growing up happens to take place in Poland in the 1930s, and you have a weak mental constitution . . .

The innocent period of my life, when "being a Jew" was not an issue for me, was very short. It ended with the flogging my grandfather performed on me with his cane, when he heard that I was prepared to convert for the sake of a military career in the Polish army. From that moment on I have been forced to see more and to understand more. I had to painfully combine my being a Jew with Polish patriotism. I had to painfully combine Polish patriotism with my awareness of Polish anti-Semitism. I had to painfully combine Jewish patriotism with . . . disdain for Jews, disdain felt also by me.

Jewish self-disdain is an old syndrome. This disdain was first passed on to me by my mother and my Aunt Dora, when they forbade me behaviors they considered "Jewish" (for instance, talking loudly or gesturing), and then I educated myself about it by reading the Polish press and listening to Polish jokes about the Jews. All around there were anti-Semitic caricatures on posters, anti-Semitic parodies in the daily newspapers and weeklies, anti-Semitic slogans. One breathed that air! And out of this grew the repulsive and yet very suggestive stereotype of a Jew—sycophantic, cowardly, false, a Jew without dignity—so that even grown-up, intelligent people often succumbed to the power of that stereotype. All the more so a child, a child fascinated by the Polish ideal of a knight-patriot.

I was twelve years old when I realized how deeply the subconscious anti-Jewish biases had struck root in me. This was revealed as a result of a school assignment to write a paper on a topic of my choice. I decided to create a portrait of a Jew and to rely on consciously chosen literary conventions. My Jew had to be funny; had to speak in a funny, nongrammatical way; had to wear a funny, traditional Jewish overcoat; had to have funny earlocks.

The paper was a success. I sustained a uniform tone; my Jewish teachers gave me an A; my parents were proud that I could control my style in such a mature way. It was only my Aunt Manya—my beloved Aunt Manya—who had noticed what later became quite obvious to me as well: "Following a certain convention you arrived at anti-Semitism. You repeated the anti-Semitic stereotype. What you have written has nothing to do with your real experiences."

That was true. The only traditional Jews I knew were Jankiel, my grandmother's brother, and a carpenter employed by the Jewish Hospital in the Czyste neighborhood. I liked them both very much and had no intention of ridiculing them. But the stereotype overshadowed my view of reality.

How did I deal with these biases being a Jew and interacting almost exclusively with Jews? Well, one usually handles such issues on the subconscious level. My anti-Jewish sentiments were directed toward the Jews I knew least—the traditional Jews, the religiously orthodox ones (they were most often the subject of anti-Jewish caricatures), while I identified myself with the Jewish intelligentsia, of whom there were plenty all around me. Although they, too, appeared in anti-Semitic caricatures (as neurotic intellectuals), these caricatures, apparently, had no impact on my attitude.

Most painful for me—a child brought up on Polish literature and the cult of honorable combat—was the stereotypical view about the passivity and the submissiveness of the Jewish nation. For a while I believed this view conformed to the truth, and the thought that I belonged to a nation of cowards generated terrible shame in me. Fortunately, I was freed from that shame by the Jewish Scouts' organization in my school. My leaders, just a few years older than I, combined Polish and Jewish patriotisms in a most unusual way, developing Jewish pride in us, the Jewish children. "When someone in the street says to you: 'You stupid Jew,' don't let him!" they taught us. "When they want to beat you up, pull out the ruler from your backpack and fight!" They had implanted the ethos of a proud Jew in me so deeply that at the beginning of the war, before the ghetto was created, when on several occasions I was attacked by Polish hooligans, I always reacted so strongly that at times it bordered on stupidity. I was afraid, but I attacked. The mere thought that I might convey that a Jew was weaker than they were, or not as good, filled me with disgust.

The Jews whom I knew and respected hated the stereotype of a passive and cowardly Jew. This hatred, by the way, was one of the sources of Zionism—the Zionist dream that Jews, like other nations, have their own land, farmers, workers, criminals, and soldiers. And—that they know how to fight. Because of his Jewish pride, my father, for instance, was once severely roughed up by "Endeks," the xenophobic Polish Nationalist Democrats. "We are looking for Jews. Do you happen to be one?" they yelled at him when he was riding in a horse drawn coach. "And what if I am?" he snapped back. That's when they beat him up.

My mother also liked the ethos of Jewish pride. She was afraid I might get hurt and told me to avoid conflicts with the Poles. She was not trying to talk me into humility but suggested an attitude of loftiness, like: "Aristotle will not fight with a bull." By not responding to aggressive remarks I was to feel superior, wiser. I often felt that way. I remember being in the street (I must have been around eleven years old), and the Polish tram drivers telling me that Jews don't believe in God at all. I decided I would agree with them. "Yes, we are materialists. We only look for profit. What else matters but profit?" I uttered this nonsense, looking them boldly in the eyes. I took intellectual revenge upon them, confirming their ignorance and stupidity.

The attitude of superiority toward anti-Semites was a form of inner defense for me. And although I didn't feel physically threatened in my childhood (some adult always walked me to school; I was not allowed out of the house before Catholic holidays when more thugs than usual tended to be in the streets), yet I knew, I've almost always known, that there are people who hate me only because I am a Jew. Once (I was about eight then), when I bent down in a store to help pick up some coins a man had dropped, he yelled: "Don't touch my money, you dirty piece of shit!" (even the saleslady got scared). I understood then and there that this man hated Jews. I felt the same way on another occasion. I was waiting for a train to Zakopane with a Polish lady, my Aunt Manya's acquaintance, and one of the high school or college students passing by took a look at me and yelled: "It reeks of garlic here!"

It was at moments like these that the thought "people who say such things are of an inferior kind" brought me back to an equilibrium. And it was then that in my mind I repeated to myself: "Fools. Stupid anti-Semites. Stupid Polish anti-Semites. Stupid Poles."

When my mother told me that I had to take an admission test to a good state-owned Polish high school, I was seriously alarmed. To go to school with Poles?! Was I to abandon the safe Jewish environment, my Jewish friends with whom I attended school for six years, my sensible and gentle Jewish teachers? Was I to enter the cold world? I expected the worst in a Polish school: alienation, anti-Semitism, and severe discipline. Additionally, I was anxious because I had to pass the exam with very high marks, since there was a *numerus clausus* and only 5 percent of Jews were accepted.

My mother insisted: "If you graduate from a Polish high school, you'll have a better chance to get admitted to the university!" Finally, I gave in and in June of 1939 I passed the admission test to the so-called "tram drivers'" high school on Młynarska Street. Whether I really did well on the test or whether I was accepted because of my senator grandfather's pull, I'll never know. I do know, however, that the day I stepped over the threshold of the new school, dressed in an elegant uniform (paid for by my other grandfather and Aunt Dora), was extremely stressful for me.

Postponed because of the outbreak of the war, classes didn't begin till October 1939 and ended just a few weeks later, when the Germans closed all high schools in Poland. When that occurred, I breathed a sigh of relief. I would not have lasted in that horrible environment

much longer: a class of forty, many dull students, blockheads held over
from the previous year, (only one more Jew was in the class, the rest
were Poles), terrible noise and chaos in the corridors during recesses,
frequent fights, aggression, very painful slingshot attacks with card-
board pellets as ammunition.

With what longing I thought then about my old Jewish school on
Rysia Street (the famous "Our School" run by Mrs. Olderfeld, whom
my parents considered almost a creature of a higher order). There,
fights among boys had amounted mainly to chasing; there, classes consisted of fifteen to twenty students; there, we had joint classes with
girls, even gym classes and locker rooms—something probably impossible in any Polish school. . . .

Relations between teachers and students in my high school were
rather bizarre. Essentially, there were no relations but terrible stiffness
and distance. In my old Jewish school we approached teachers after
classes about various matters, addressing them familiarly by their first
names, Mr. Zygmunt, Mr. Mieczyslaw. . . . There was warmth. But
here, even when one didn't understand a lecture, one didn't dare to ask!
And all you would say was: "Yes, Mr. Professor; yes, Mr. Professor."

I suffered because of my Jewishness from the very beginning. Some
blockhead held over from the previous year pushed me and called me
a kike. I talked back, he jumped on me, and that's how it began. The
same happened on the second day; the same on the third. It was my
Polish class teacher who saved me. He took it so much to heart when
my mother came running to school to complain that he assembled all
the students in the classroom and said solemnly: "Nothing like that
must happen here! Whoever attacks people of other faiths will be severely punished."

From then on I was left in peace. Yet, I didn't feel comfortable
among those students. Although some were nice (I remember the first
day someone addressed me as "colleague" and I responded likewise; I
liked it a lot that we acted so grown-up), but these people were total
strangers to me! Once, when the teacher gave us an assignment to
write on the topic "What happens on your way home from school?" I
was shocked to discover what my classmates wrote. One was passing
some church and saw the Virgin Mary with tears in her eyes or some
other miracle. . . . For me, educated in a modern Jewish school, where
we were inculcated with the cult of rationality and respect for West-

ern democracies (at the sound of "The Marseillaise" we spontaneously jumped to attention), the idea that some picture could cry was totally fantastic! What the hell! What kinds of minds did they have?! We lived jointly in the same world, but they saw things that to me were total superstitions! And even if this weeping picture was merely a literary convention, I wondered why they chose *such* a convention.

Yes. We were divided by religious and class differences. They were educated in Catholic-nationalistic schools and came mostly from working-class families; I was a graduate of an elite Jewish school, where students were both atheists and believers, but where no attention was paid to ritual. Almost from early childhood on I considered religion to be outdated, because in synagogues I saw mainly Jews with earlocks, wearing caftans, Jews distant from my life. When later I discovered that the Poles also had their own religion, different from ours, I treated their religiosity also with a distrustful distance.

In those days—at the beginning of the German occupation but before the ghetto was decreed—I already genuinely disliked Poles, primarily because of their physical threat. The war emboldened the anti-Semites, and one heard repeatedly that here and there someone was attacked by Poles. At the beginning of the war, the Germans simply robbed Jewish homes. A German officer took a set of surgical instruments from my uncle who was a doctor. And it was said of the Poles, mostly those from the *lumpenproletariat,* that they were having fun beating up "Yids." Once, trying to get on a tram, I myself was pushed aside by some boy (so that my book fell out from under my arm). He yelled, "Where are you shoving yourself, Jew?" On another occasion, some youngsters on Skierniewicka Street began pounding me when I responded sharply to their remark: "Look, a kike is coming!" Polish hooligans appeared even more threatening to me than the Germans, because, in the streets, the Germans only attacked Orthodox Jews, those with earlocks. The Poles, however, recognized a Jew in me. And they wanted to show me how worthless I was.

As a result of all these experiences, something strange began to develop with regard to my attitude toward the Jewish national idea and Jewish religion. I felt somehow closer to Jewishness. I began to think with a certain respect about religious Jews, living according to tradition. I recognized in them both national dignity and heroism in sustaining Jewish culture. "There's something to it"—I thought—"to being a religious Jew, treating Jewishness with consistency, going to synagogue, observing the Jewish dietary laws of *kashrut,* and even wearing earlocks." And at the same time, I realized that for me—an atheist, a boy aligned with the assimilating Jewish intelligentsia— that attitude was totally unattainable. Even identification with all the European secular Jews was impossible for me! All the more so religious Jews, who were like an alien nation: strange, not understood, almost as distant as the Poles . . .

In no way could I identify emotionally with the Jewish nation, even at the moment when I realized that it would truly make sense to do so.

※

3

I have always felt detached from life. My overprotective mother separated me very effectively from the dangerous world. Now, however, when the war broke out, the sense of isolation gnawed at me even more. My contacts with children were limited to a small group in clandestine schooling; there were no girls around me; I didn't engage in any sport. Growing up and entering the world in a normal way was not accessible to me. Because the world—the social world—wasn't there. So I retreated to live in my own world. It was a bit of a dream life.

My father died just before the outbreak of the war, on the day the Ribbentrop-Molotov pact was announced. He had a stroke and died suddenly. Mother had always told me to be quiet when he was resting after work because he had high blood pressure. She was afraid he might die. As a consequence of her fears I began to fear she might die, too.

Some Poles who had worked with my father, Mr. Skoczek and Mr. Barański, came to our house to pay their respects. Mr. Skoczek cried. He was my father's closest associate. His family lived in a village near Kielce, and he would always bring us some tasty country food.

There was a funeral with lots of people, acceptance of countless condolences, flowers, wreaths, and my mother and I, arm in arm, in this enormous funeral procession.

And soon afterward, the war broke out. We were listening to the radio. One day they announced: "This is radio Warsaw, Kraków, Poznań." A few days later: "This is radio Warsaw and Kraków." And then only "This is radio Warsaw." In no time there was no government. Only Starzyński, the president of Warsaw, remained. And we could hear the artillery fire.

My grandfather from Tłomackie Street, the senator, escaped east with his son Lolek. He left my grandmother behind. My mother and I decided to move in with her, but at the end of September the bombing began and grandfather's house burned down . . . along with my childhood.

I was attached to my grandfather's place like a cat! I had spent so much time there. I had read so many books there. I had so much fun being in this elegant six-room apartment on Tłomackie Street!

The house burned slowly. The fire brigade didn't want to come. My mother and Uncle Marian carried out the furniture, the clothing, the paintings.

I felt I was losing my mooring. Now anything could happen.

After the arrival of the Germans, we went back to live in my father's hospital-owned apartment in the Czyste neighborhood. My grandmother, my little Aunt Marysia (my mother's sister) and her husband Marian moved in with us because their house in Leszno Street had also been destroyed. Following father's death, we felt insecure in his apartment, since we could have been evicted at any moment. But since there was a period of interregnum in the hospital—the director escaped, and the German administration hadn't taken over yet—my mother exploited this cleverly and took over my father's professional duties. She began managing the hospital without asking anybody's permission. And that's how it remained.

I had a lot of freedom now, since mother was completely absorbed by work in the hospital. Earlier, she had dedicated all her attention to raising me and controlling me. She steered me so precisely that she even developed a reading list for each year of my life (I was to read Żeromski's *Ashes* only after my fourteenth birthday!). Now, she hardly concerned herself with me at all! I could read whatever I wanted, go wherever I wanted, do whatever I wanted. I became a free man, all the more so when, after a few weeks of German occupation, my dismal "tram drivers'" high school closed.

I would leave the apartment and ride the trams. I would go here and there to look at the city of Warsaw. The streets were dark, repulsive, often ruined. They totally lost their warm prewar atmosphere. I was plagued by a sense of time passing. With the death of my father, my old life was severed—wham, with one blow. I kept remembering my old friends. I saw Stefan from time to time, but I wondered what the others were doing. What was Staś Głowiński, the best student in our

Jewish school, doing? Or Rafek Kazanowicz, whose family was from Lithuania? Or Jurek Bronowski, an awesome boy, who was superb at imitating the peasants' speech? Or girls: Klara Kantif, Irenka Baumgardten, Anka Lewin? Or Lidia Kalafiol, my first childhood love. (It was a love "bestowed" on me . . . I always glanced at her fondly until some other girl said to me: "You've fallen in love with Lidia," so I thought maybe that was true. After classes, Stefan Wandel and I began to follow Lidia on her way from school. We followed her together because we did everything together, so if I had fallen in love, Stefan also had to fall in love.)

I missed them. I read a lot: Turgenev, Chekhov, Tolstoy, Bertrand Russell's *An Outline of Philosophy,* the Encyclopedists, books on physics. I would return from my tram voyages freezing, fling myself on my small sofa and immerse myself in books and contemplation. Is the human world ruled by laws as inevitable as those of the physical world? Are English boys different from me? Who am I? Who will I be in the future? Is fame an important thing?

I often went over to my beloved Aunt Manya's (my father's sister's) home to talk to her. She taught me English, loaned me books from her enormous library, listened to me. She had an exceptional gift for listening! And she knew how to converse in a way that, without hurting my feelings, she would point out all the errors of my reasoning.

I roamed around the city with Stefan. We talked about ideologies, about the order of things, about sex. Stefan was considerably more mature than I was in all respects, in matters of sex, too. I recall that when our prewar Jewish class reached puberty, and there were whispers, the girls were giggling, I had no clue at all what it was all about! In an attempt to maintain the role of the class ironist, I started making equivocal remarks, without myself understanding their meaning. The girls would burst out laughing, so would the boys, who were rather dumb. One teacher decided to summon my mother to school because she had concluded I was provoking an unhealthy atmosphere. And it was then that Stefan had to explain everything to me, to enlighten me.

This prewar period seemed so remote to me, so very desirable. I missed it terribly. . . .

One day the dream about recreating the prewar world suddenly became plausible. It occurred to me—or my mother, or perhaps Aunt Manya—that we should organize clandestine schooling. I took to the idea with a truly abnormal zeal. I located classmates, talked to their mothers; I was building the old world out of fragments. My nostalgic trips all over Warsaw suddenly acquired a new meaning.

I managed to bring together a group of five children. The rest disappeared. They had fled beyond the river Bug to the Soviet occupied zone, or changed addresses. My mother and Aunt Manya engaged two teachers—Ms. Zofia Levi for the humanities and Ms. Halina for biology and math. And we began. I was embarking on a way of experiencing life in an unusually intellectual manner.

Our teachers were truly exceptional—sensitive, highly educated, inspirational. Never before have I derived so much satisfaction from learning. Influenced by Ms. Halina's lessons, I purchased Darwin's *The Origin of Species;* I contemplated the history of the earth, the essence of nature, of the universe.

It was a harsh winter, as I recall. We would come to the daily classes frozen. With fingers stiff from the cold, we would take out the books and a lesson would begin, a discussion, our entry into the fascinating intellectual world. In no other school, in no subsequent group have I ever learned as much as I have from these two unusual women. Theirs was a true labor of love.

My family was preoccupied with everyday worries. One had to procure food. The supplies of flour and groats garnered up by my grandmother in the first days of September (purchased when farmers would still come to Warsaw with their horse-drawn wagons)—burned up on Tłomackie Street. Food was rationed. Prices on the black market were astronomical. I remember my grandmother's horror—"butter costs twenty-five zlotys today!" "And how much was it before the war?" I asked. "Two zlotys!"

We lived on my mother's income and the soups she brought from the hospital. When that wasn't enough, grandmother, with a sigh, would pull out another piece of her jewelry to be sold. We knew we could survive like that a year or two. But what would happen next? Thoughts about the future instilled fear in my family.

Mother was fighting to retain her position in the hospital. After the period of interregnum, others emerged who were interested in her job. She created then an entire staff of allies (among them, I remember, was a Dr. Munwez, who was probably a bit in love with my mother), and she spoke about her opponents with great hatred and contempt. And I criticized her. I told her she was being subjective and pigheaded. Although I knew the survival of our entire family depended on her job, I would proclaim that she should attempt greater objectivity in judging people.

I was a *Schoengeist,* a beautiful soul, detached from reality. I read books and organized clandestine schooling. Actually, nothing else was expected of me. I had always been separated from practical matters. "You don't know how, you couldn't, you need help," my mother argued when she wanted to limit my independence. She had repeated "you are impractical" so many times that I no longer even heard it.

Indeed, now that the war broke out and I was already twelve years old, I could have helped my family in some way. But the "you are impractical" was so strongly implanted in me that I continued to believe that to worry about what I would eat and where I would sleep was up to others. My world consisted of books, dreams, discussions. It was a world of abstractions, a world of intellectual pursuits. I immersed myself in it deeper and deeper. And increasingly I delved into books to separate myself from the real world.

Wandering around Warsaw was sometimes dangerous. But the danger was easily reduced. One might get beaten up by Polish hooligans, but they could be identified by their *lumpenproletarian* looks and one could get out of their way in time. One might be attacked by the Germans, but at the beginning of the war their aggression was directed at Orthodox Jews, with earlocks, so I did not feel threatened. One might get in trouble for not wearing an armband (we often walked without one—my peers and I—because that gave us the relish of childish rebellion); one might also get a good rubbing for provocative behavior (once I ripped off a German propaganda poster and was very disappointed when a Pole, a passerby who saw what I had done, instead of praising me, reprimanded me—and justly so—for my stupidity).

But now and then something truly unpleasant would happen. On one occasion, when I was jaywalking, a "navy blue" policeman approached me and said: "Where are you shuffling, little kike?" "You could address me with a bit more civility!" I responded. "Is that sooo? Just you wait. You'll see how I'll address you!" He twisted my arm and dragged me to the police station.

It all happened suddenly. I was hurled into a circle of thieves, prostitutes, and drunks; into a cell with people who spoke and behaved in a strange way. My intellectual world of books and discussions vanished. What occurred was a disturbance in the self-evident order of reality as I had seen it until then!

I was in a state of panic. Not because I was in danger of something horrible happening to me but because such an unexpected thing could occur in my life. I have a deep need for a sense of order in my world. When that order is disturbed, I get totally lost in my helplessness.

At the police station, I also had an incident with a cop who made me sign my alleged confession without even letting me read it. Like a fool, I signed it. Fortunately, some acquaintance, who had seen me being arrested, notified my mother and she—completely distraught from worry—found me the next day and bailed me out. That's how I was pulled out of that nightmare.

Unquestionably, the atmosphere all around me was one of fear, fear and insecurity. People didn't know what to expect. Although at the beginning the situation wasn't so bad, because the Germans were busy organizing life under their occupation, we certainly knew—we'd known almost all along—that their program was anti-Semitic and that something must happen to the Jews.

It began in a matter of weeks, with robberies of Jewish homes. The Germans came to the apartments of more affluent Jews and took things they liked. Sometimes they behaved in a cool and civil manner; sometimes they were brutal; sometimes they pulled up in enormous trucks and took away all of people's possessions. There was nothing one could do about it. After the first attempts of Jewish protests, when the news spread that those who had gone to German offices to complain were beaten or arrested, we understood that we had to succumb.

In November of 1939, Warsaw was flooded with Jewish refugees from Poland's western territories, which by then had been incorporated into the Reich. The refugees could be seen everywhere. They came in horse-drawn wagons, on trains, and also on foot. They told tales of horror: that the Germans had chased them out of their towns, giving them an hour or less to leave their homes; that they beat them brutally and occasionally even shot Jews.

Poles, some Poles (the intelligentsia, state employees), were also chased out of those territories, but it was done quite differently. They were allowed time to prepare for the departure and permitted to take their belongings. From the very beginning of the occupation it was clear that the fates of the Poles and Jews would be different.

In our home, quite early, one used to hear: "We won't survive this war." But what was really the point of declaring that I find difficult to say today. I don't think that then, in the fall of 1939, anyone among the people around me anticipated the total annihilation of Jews. People thought: "Things are bad, very bad, horrible—but had not Jews survived many dark moments in their history?"

The order was issued to the Jews of Warsaw to wear an armband with a Star of David. This was followed promptly by the edict that Jews between the age of fourteen and sixty were obliged to work. The Germans would come to the Jewish Council and say: we need a hundred Jews to build a road, three hundred Jews to clean the rubble. The first labor camps, ostensibly for volunteers, were organized. An engineer who worked in my mother's hospital sent his twenty-year-old son to such a camp for a while (there were some conflicts between them). But when he wanted to bring him back, because the son had been writing desperate letters, it turned out that it wasn't possible. The allegedly voluntary camp was simply a trap.

In mid-November of 1939 there was talk of German plans to concentrate Jews in the region of Lublin. The question *why* was often discussed by my family. People aren't stupid, after all. It was known that the Germans had some plans concerning us, but what these were we couldn't imagine at all.

Barbed wires and the sign "Jewish Quarter: Typhus Hazard!" appeared in Warsaw. These wires—and in short order, walls—had open passages; they didn't close anything. But they looked very threatening and had a strong psychological impact.

News reached us from other parts of Poland: there was a ghetto in Łódź; there was a ghetto in Piotrków; there was a ghetto here and a ghetto there. One day, in the summer of 1940, little Aunt Marysia brought us the news she obtained from an acquaintance in the Jewish Council: "There will be a ghetto in Warsaw, but its boundaries haven't been determined yet."

"There will be a ghetto in Warsaw." But what was the meaning of "There will be a ghetto in Warsaw"?

One day Poles who collaborated with the German police came to our house. They were looking for my senator grandfather (who had escaped to Vilna). My mother and Aunt Marysia offered tea to these men to minimize the tension. A conversation ensued and suddenly Aunt Marysia asked: "And how are the Poles reacting to the crowding of the Jews in the ghetto?" (At that time the ghetto was already beginning to be formed.) And then one of those secret service agents explained it to us so smoothly: "For us, Poles, it's a good thing. The city is cleaner. Those dirty Jews are no longer in Warsaw."

I don't remember if this hurt our feelings very much. Our emotional ties with the Poles were growing progressively weaker. Before the war, it was always important to us what the Poles did. My father and the senator grandfather constantly discussed this or that law introduced by the Poles. But now, when it was known that in the occupied Poland the status of Jews and Poles would be different, the Polish and the Jewish worlds began distancing themselves from each other.

We knew that the Poles were organizing some resistance movement, that there were already some victims, some executions. But we were far from them. We were getting ready for the confrontation with our own fate, a lonely confrontation. And now what was important to us was not what the Poles were doing, but what the Germans were doing, what the Germans would do to us.

Were we prepared for life in the ghetto? Of course not! Can one store enough food for three, four years? The Germans were winning the war! They spoke triumphantly about a one-thousand-year Reich! True, my mother entrusted my senator grandfather's valuable paintings to a Polish acquaintance for safekeeping. But that was all one could do under the circumstances. The only sensible attitude toward the prospect of a ghetto was: "We'll go there and we'll see. Either it will be possible to live in a ghetto or not. But at this time, when nobody knows what the ghetto is like, one cannot prepare for it."

The time until the establishment of the ghetto—and then in the ghetto—was a period of total instability. Normal people make some plans—for next month or year. Now they lived in absolute suspense. No one knew what tomorrow would bring.

Many people had escaped a long time ago beyond the river Bug to the Soviet-occupied zone. But we remained. My mother's job gave her a sense of security. Besides, Mother didn't trust the Communists. "Let's be thankful that we were occupied by the Germans and not the Russians," she used to say at the beginning of the German occupation. Later, when the ghetto was already being established, it was too late to escape.

While my family worried about our survival, I read Descartes. Now I recognize a kind of anomaly in this, but the horror of the war did not reach me at the beginning of the occupation, nor even later. And although on some deep level I must have been conscious of the gravity of the situation, I did not think about it. I treated the words "we won't survive this war" as typical adult exaggeration.

I have often wondered how I attained this deep sense of physical security. I think that my mother, who controlled and protected me so much in my childhood, must have created an irrational impression in me that someone would always ensure my welfare. I lived as if some security umbrella were spread over me. All around me were fear, uncertainty, situations full of menace, while my emotional life then was centered on thoughts of my future: who would I become? How would I distinguish myself? How would I gain fame? I wanted to be a scientist and make a major discovery.

I recall that in the late autumn of 1940, when everybody was already in the ghetto (the closed ghetto) and only our hospital was still on the Aryan side and awaiting transfer, I would go out in the evenings to the hospital garden and just walk around for an hour or two. I did that every day, almost obsessively, until one day Mother said to me: "Pretty soon people will start laughing at you!"

A year and a half ago—I was thinking then—I had played ball in this very garden with the children of the blue-collar workers of the hospital. When the war broke out, however, they started participating in the grown-ups' worries about economic survival and we stopped playing. A year ago, I was organizing clandestine schooling, but our wonderful group lasted only till the summer vacation. The following fall we did not succeed in convening the group. A few months before I used to play Ping-Pong with Stefan Wandel. This Ping-Pong (a net stretched over the table in Stefan's home) was the only kind of sport accessible to us during the war—and now Stefan was already in the ghetto, and we were to move there when the hospital would be transferred.

I was alone. I was becoming outré. I had no peers around me.

I was becoming sensitive to the presence of women, but there were no girls around me.

Under normal circumstances, children expand the circle of their friends at that age. They meet new people at high school. They aspire to independence. And I? What could I do? While the hospital was still on the Aryan side, its employees and patients could not even step out beyond the fence!

Books, dreams, and evening walks in the garden, that was all I had.

The first year of my abnormal existence was coming to an end.

4

People think the ghetto was like in the movies: constant, relentless terror. But it wasn't like that at all. We were always surrounded by terror, but we led normal lives right alongside it. Flirting went on in the ghetto, romances, concerts, theatrical performances. People went to a restaurant, while behind the restaurant someone was dying. The normal and the abnormal intertwined repeatedly.

When the Germans finally established the borders of the "Closed Quarter" (more or less the area of the former Jewish Quarter), a nervousness spread over Warsaw. Jews who lived outside the future ghetto exchanged apartments with Poles living in that area. Those who were unable to exchange apartments received some lodgings in the ghetto from the Jewish Council. All of this was being done in a hurry because the Germans allowed only three or four weeks for the move.

We did not participate in this bustle. As the financial director of the hospital, mother was entitled to an apartment in the ghetto provided by the hospital. We had a different worry: Would the Germans transfer the hospital to the ghetto or not. If they didn't do so, we would be a kind of sealed Jewish island on the Aryan side.

Time passed. The Germans closed the ghetto, but the entire hospital (we still could not leave its premises) continued to wait for the transfer. We were like prisoners. In the evenings, which dragged endlessly, we constantly played Monopoly. When the day of the move finally came, my mother hired some furniture moving firm, and we packed everything up and transferred inside the walls.

The ghetto street made a strange impression on me: crowds, noise, commotion, people in tatters, begging children. And one could hear Yiddish everywhere, a language I didn't understand, of course.

We entered our new apartment on Leszno Street. Although it consisted of three rooms, they were dark, small, and gloomy. Right away I missed our sunny apartment in the Czyste neighborhood. I got this sinking feeling that I would have to live in this place now, and who knew how long.

I was very depressed during the first days in the ghetto, but at the same time my energy level went up. After days of being locked up in the hospital, I could now walk freely in the streets, meet Stefan, play Ping-Pong with him. I was no longer alone.

One day I came to a strange realization—that I felt safe in the streets of the ghetto. This was a new, very concrete sense of physical security. Everybody in the ghetto felt it as a great relief. Earlier, in occupied Warsaw, before it was separated by the ghetto wall, we probably did not realize how vigilant and tense we had been. That tension was totally gone. We were alone. There were no Poles, no Germans (except guards at the ghetto gates), no anti-Semitic provocations awaited us, no robbery, no rape. Jewish policemen attended to order. And although there was death all around us, because from the very beginning people were starving in the ghetto (usually refugees from other ghettos), one did not feel physically threatened. As never before.

During this initial period, the ghetto was even safer for the Jews than the Aryan side was for the Poles. Poles on the Aryan side risked capture, repression, executions, while we risked nothing. Only occasionally did the German administration demand a large quantity of furs from the Jewish Council or impose a high tax. Sometimes a German soldier would shoot from the wall just for fun. But these were rare incidents.

Life in my new home was slowly falling into a regular rhythm. Mother, as usual, rushed to the hospital. Uncle Marian, little Aunt Marysia's husband, went to the Jewish Council offices (he had some minor job there). I went to classes offered by Ms. Zofia Levi and Ms. Halina (Stefan and I managed to find them in the ghetto), then to English lessons with Aunt Manya or French lessons with a Jewish woman from Russia (a very intelligent person, a friend of one of my distant aunts). At home, I did homework in physics and math. I studied Latin. I read.

I remember borrowing from Mr. Rozen *Swann's Way* by Proust. I remember having read Rousseau's *Confessions*. I remember having begun reading Romain Rolland, Malraux. . . .

What else do I remember? Why do I remember so little of the first winter in the ghetto?

In those days, the song "Geb ub dee boneh" (Yiddish for "Give Up the Ration Coupon") was sung everywhere in the streets. The food ration was something symbolic—about five pounds of bread per month and about twelve ounces of sugar (occasionally also some potatoes and marmalade). Those who had money bought food on the black market. Those who didn't, well . . .

The words "we won't survive this war" were acquiring a new and very concrete meaning. There were more and more beggars in the streets, more and more corpses thrown onto the sidewalks by families who could not afford to bury them.

We, however, were not starving. There were two incomes (mother's and uncle's); mother brought soups from the hospital; grandma sold jewelry.

Our friends, likewise, were not starving. People from our social stratum—doctors, lawyers, teachers—did not go under for quite a while. There was starvation all around us, but we were not touched by it. Our life followed its own course. The grown-ups worried about economic survival; the children attended classes.

Today everybody wonders how one could have lived so normally then, alongside death and with the prospect of death. Intelligent people understood, to be sure, that the money would end and everything would end. And yet, in the spring of 1941—that is, precisely when the total German domination was about to happen—my mother, whose clarity of mind could not be denied, found a new clandestine school (run by former teachers of the Jewish "Spójnia" [Union]) high school, which issued real graduation diplomas or certificates of completion of a grade. And later, in the spring of 1942, when there were numerous signs that the ghetto would soon be exterminated, mother tried to persuade me to take private lessons during the summer, so I could skip one grade of high school. What for?

Aunt Dora organized individual private lessons with distinguished specialists for her son Jędruś, a year younger than I. Jędruś studied biology with the famous scientist Szymon Tenenbaum and, in fact, did complete two grades in a year. What for?

Other mothers had similar ambitions. It was because of them that the Jewish intelligentsia was able to support itself by teaching children. The concern for children's education was as common in the ghetto then as was the saying "we won't survive this war."

Is this a contradiction? Perhaps. But the habit of thinking about the future and a sense of the congruity of life are deeply rooted in people. During this initial period in the ghetto, that sense wasn't yet totally destroyed. It was seriously wounded but not destroyed. Life, despite sickness and death, had its rhythm, was stable. When one eats fairly well, when one lives in hygienic conditions (we had a bathroom with hot running water), when one has a relative sense of physical security, then, even despite common sense, one's thoughts run toward the future. "It's not very likely that all will survive," everybody thought. "But some individuals might . . . Perhaps we will be the ones to overcome hunger? And perhaps this German system will relent somewhat?"

Two foreign languages were being taught in the clandestine classes: German and French. The majority of parents chose German for their children—the language of the future. The Germans were conquering Europe then. They were winning. A horrible world totally ruled by them was emerging—the *Neue Ordnung,* a new order.

Well, but aren't some of us likely to survive? And won't there be some place for Jews in the new order? Even if we don't survive, perhaps our children will. They will have to live somehow, to manage somehow . . . They have to be prepared, educated. One has to think about their future.

In June 1941 the Soviet-German war broke out. This was the miracle that was supposed to happen. When the loudspeaker in the street blared out the news I rushed home, yelling "This is the final act. The Germans are fighting on two fronts now!"

People were excited. At long last there was a potential chance for some change. Earlier, the war was like an endless tunnel; no one could stop Hitler. But now something new was emerging: a confrontation. If Germany won't conquer Russia, then Russia will conquer Germany.

For the time being, however, the Germans pushed forward and

refugees from the territories occupied by them—Vilna, Lwów, Barano-
wicze, Lida—started pouring into Warsaw. Unfortunately, they didn't
bring hope; they brought dread. It was from them that the Warsaw
ghetto found out about the systematic extermination in the eastern
territories of Poland; about the terrible special divisions dedicated exclusively to capturing and shooting Jews; about the horrible pogroms
perpetrated by Germans and Ukrainians.

Yet it is hard to believe in extermination. Although it was clear that
the Germans had bad intentions, the Jews of Warsaw constantly de-
luded themselves that their stable ghetto would not end. "Perhaps
the murders are taking place only in the countryside," my little Aunt
Marysia, my mother's sister, consoled herself, "and in the big cities
they may concentrate us, starve us, but they will take no action." But
a moment later she would sigh: "Oh, we won't survive this war."

Such mood swings were characteristic of the majority of people I
knew then.

I still did not sense the threat. Despite my good grasp of the situation,
I banished the thought that I or my family might be annihilated. The
only thing I was afraid of was typhus. In the summer of 1941, four
to five thousand people died in Warsaw monthly (one percent of the
ghetto population every month). One almost stumbled on corpses on
the sidewalks. I always attempted to walk in such a way as to avoid
touching anyone or brushing against anyone. I remember that once,
when accidentally some unknown girl in tatters leaned on me, I
walked for several hours terrified that I had lice on me.

My mother arranged for an official job for me at the hospital telephone switchboard (three hours on duty, sometimes in the afternoon
and sometimes in the evening). The telephone switchboard office became a center of my social life. Ludwik Asz, whose mother was a doctor in the hospital and whose father, who had died before the war, had
been a conductor and composer, worked there. (Sometimes Ludwik and
I would discuss physics, genetics, the cosmos, philosophy, or literature
for hours.) Marian Lewenfisz and Michał Dorfman (whom I liked very
much) would also come there. After work we would play Ping-Pong together or just walk around the ghetto or listen to concerts.

At that time I became fascinated with music. It was in the ghetto
that I attended my first real concert. Aunt Marysia took me to the

movie house Femina, where Jewish musicians, who had formed an orchestra, performed every week. I was so moved by that concert, so elated, that for two days I couldn't talk about anything else. My very musical family considered that an affectation, but I was firm in my resolve. I had to go to every concert, every Saturday.

My friends and I would talk a lot about girls, but I knew none. Across the street from my apartment two teenage girls often sunbathed in their window, and I always gazed at them, trying to catch the moment when they changed their clothes.

Once, Mother told me that her friends' daughters—Hanna Kon and Jasia Lewinson—would like to listen to some music. She asked me to organize a soiree and play some records for them. I agreed. I also invited Ludwik, and we listened to Beethoven. I sat stiff as a stick. I fell in love with Jasia at once; I would walk past her house and wait for her to come out, totally mortified. I had no clue how to approach her.

One day at supper, Mother mentioned that a friend of hers from the hospital had said on some occasion with a sigh: "I feel terribly sorry for the children in the ghetto!"

This made me wonder. Why did he feel sorry for us? And it was only after a while that I realized my life would be quite different if there were no ghetto! I would have friends, perhaps also girlfriends; I'd make plans for the future; I'd be getting ready for the university. Until then, I hadn't thought about it at all. Nor did I feel very unhappy. Basically, my crippled, stunted life of a ghetto teenager seemed quite normal to me.

In October of 1941 my grandfather from Kiliński Street, my father's father, died of typhus. He was a religious man. He used to pray in the synagogue on Saturdays. He caught some lice there and fell sick. Aunt Dora cried: 'Father, I told you so many times not to go to the synagogue!"

Grandfather from Kiliński Street was my wise, kind, beloved grandpa. His attitude toward the world was bright and full of simplicity. I always welcomed my grandfather with a kiss. On the day he fell sick, I kissed him as usual and I got worried. He was sitting and being so morose that I kissed him again, saying: "Grandpa, you are running a fever!" A few days later he was dead.

Soon after grandpa's death my French teacher, the intelligent Russian Jewess, died of typhus.

Then Zofia Levi died of cancer.

At the end of June 1942, my Aunt Dora died of a stroke. Death was nearer and nearer.

Did I talk with my peers about death? No. Absolutely not. Politics, military maneuvers, that we did talk about. But not about what concerned us so immediately. Even when we discussed existential issues—the meaning or brevity of life—it was never in the context of our ghetto experience but always in abstract terms and in connection with the books we had read.

The same was true of our clandestine classes. I recall a lot of laughter, games, jokes, but no conversations about death. We did not talk about it with the teachers either. Neither with Ms. Zofia Levi nor with Ms. Halina (when the former was still alive); not in the new class where my history and Latin teacher, the very intelligent Mr. Kirszbaum (he was also a musician and played in the Jewish orchestra "Femina"), who would willingly talk to me about history or politics but never about our life.

This avoidance of the subject of death was not calculated. There was no taboo, no unwritten law not to speak about it. We simply didn't. I didn't talk about it because—despite my terrible depression after my grandfather's funeral—death just didn't engage my attention to a very high degree. Today I wonder why others didn't talk about it.

Sometimes it occurs to me that perhaps I was not the only one with this kind of protective shield. Many of my peers lived like me—detached from reality, with an irrational sense of security. Where did it come from?

It's true that we didn't have to worry about physical well-being. With the exception of Stefan and Michał Dorfman, we were well off and that had some bearing. But our unconcern was more than the immaturity of pampered boys. It was more than selfishness and thoughtlessness.

What was it? I don't know. Perhaps self-defense? A defense against a nightmare? A defense of young organisms with a desire to live against an experience there was no way to experience?

In February 1942, Uncle Lolek, my mother's brother, arrived from Vilna. Shortly afterward my senator grandfather from Tłomackie

Street came back. Both of them had escaped beyond the river Bug into the Soviet zone in September of 1939. But now that the Germans had entered Vilna, my family decided to bring them back to Warsaw.

At home, the tone of our conversations changed with their arrival. Lolek was ruthless in his opinions. "Don't have any illusions! We'll all die! They'll liquidate the Jews of Warsaw as they did the Jews of Vilna, Słonim, Kobryń!"

Aunt Marysia tried to oppose him: "But they won't dare in Warsaw!" He responded: "What do you mean, they won't dare? They couldn't care less about public opinion! They'll kill us off! The only sensible move is to join the partisans!" The partisans were his obsession. "If I didn't have to take care of Father, I'd join them at once. Today! Because there's only death here!"

One day I was doing my homework, and he jumped on me: "What? You are studying the poet Słowacki? What's the point now?! Even if you survive the war, what do you think you'll do then?!" "Leave him alone. Let him be," my grandmother tried to calm him, seeing that I was totally unsettled. "Leave him alone, he is just a child. . . ." "Well, I'll enroll at the university, I'll study physics . . . ," I tried to defend myself. "I'll study physics! I'll be an intellectual!" Lolek was getting furious. "So you think that nothing will change after all this? That life will simply go on as usual?!"

Lolek was thirty, still young, and we had always liked each other very much. But something in my attitude—in my detachment from reality, in the absurdity of intellectual pursuits—must have irritated him terribly. There I was attending classes, doing homework, and not noticing at all that our world had ended, that all values had been turned upside down!

One day, when I was walking with my mother on Leszno Street, we ran into Mrs. Folfrost, my favorite teacher from the old Jewish school. She was a wise woman, calm, somewhat severe, with leftist leanings, who was raising her beautiful daughter alone. She looked like the Russian intellectual women from Chekhov's works: hair pulled up in a bun, pince-nez glasses . . .

We stopped. She looked at me warmly from behind those glasses and asked: "Are you still such a nonconformist?" She smiled. So did I. Then mother struck up a conversation with her.

I waited for them to finish talking. The sun was setting and I was looking around the ghetto. Suddenly—I have no idea what happened exactly—as I was looking at the sun, so bloody, so red . . . all at once I was beset by fear. It wasn't a normal fear! It was a cold, piercing fear. Total terror. I had absolute certainty of annihilation.

I'll perish. All of us will perish. The entire ghetto will perish. The world will be no more.

"What's the matter with you? What's going on?" My mother shook me. She got scared because I turned completely white. I didn't even attempt to explain it to her. It was as if the sun was telling me something horrible.

Was this clairvoyance? Illumination? A sudden eruption of repressed fears?

And why did it happen precisely at the moment when I was talking to Mrs. Folfrost, my wise teacher, who looked from behind her pince-nez like some beautiful, wise, intellectual woman from the pages of Chekhov?

❖

5

The safe ghetto ended in mid-April 1942. In the evenings the Gestapo policemen would drive up to some houses, pull out selected Jews, and shoot them. They left the corpses on the sidewalks. Once, during the night, a German car stopped outside our house. My senator grandfather started getting dressed. We waited. Nothing. The ignition was turned on and the car drove off. They didn't come for Grandpa.

A nervous atmosphere prevailed in the ghetto. Ukrainians in their black uniforms appeared in the streets. For the time being, they just walked around, but we knew that the Germans used the Ukrainian paramilitary formations for special tasks. Fear truly reigned supreme in our home. Grandfather, the prewar senator, was in serious danger. Had the Germans known he was in the ghetto, he would have been among the first to be shot.

My mother and grandmother walked around like time bombs. Lolek was impatient. Grandpa, as usual, maintained his cool distance, but I could see that occasionally he, too, was tense.

Only from time to time did the anxiety affect me. Generally, I remained convinced that nothing terrible would happen. I didn't want to be afraid. I had lived in the safe ghetto for too long to admit the thought that the safe ghetto was over. My friends felt the same way. One day Marian Lewenfisz came running to the telephone switchboard in a very excited state: "The Ukrainians are here! I saw them! One of them even asked me what time it was. I uncovered my watch and answered him in Ukrainian!"

Marian knew the Ukrainians were murderers because he had seen terrible Ukrainian pogroms in Lwów. (His parents were from Warsaw, but in 1939 they fled to Lwów, and when the German occupation started, they returned to Warsaw.) Marian knew the Ukrainians were thieves and thugs, yet he showed the Ukrainian his watch anyway. Like me, he was convinced that nothing terrible could happen to us in the Warsaw ghetto.

Suddenly, in the second half of July, the rumor spread that "something is going to happen at night" and one better hide. We hid in the attic. The attic was high up, it had a window, and through the window one could see a forest in the distance. I hadn't seen a forest for a year and a half! They couldn't pull me away from that window.

Nothing happened that night. We came down in the morning disoriented. What should we do? What would happen? People were milling around anxiously.

Two days later the vague rumors turned into concrete news. The edict about "mass evacuation of the Warsaw ghetto to camps in the east" was announced. All the inhabitants were to report to the Umschlagplatz and were given three kilograms of bread and a kilogram of marmalade. Those who did not come voluntarily would be brought by force and would not receive any provisions. Only one group would be allowed to stay in the ghetto legally—those who worked for the Germans and had the appropriate certificates to prove it.

People divided themselves into those who believed the Germans and those who didn't. Many went voluntarily to the Umschlagplatz immediately after the announcement, hoping there would be less hunger in the "camps in the east." It was only when it became known that the trains, which were supposed to go somewhere in the Ukraine, returned the next day with barely eaten dry loaves of bread spread all over the car floors, that everyone understood that the distant "camps in the east" were a fiction.

From the very beginning, my family didn't believe the Germans at all. We felt that evacuation meant death, although we knew nothing about the gas chambers yet. We also considered the work permits a suspect German trick, but, just in case, mother arranged for a work permit for herself and for me (as an employee of the telephone switchboard). However, my senator grandfather and Lolek, both of whom had lived with us illegally from the start, simply stayed in our apartment as before.

At that time there were no rules yet concerning hiding in the ghetto. It was dangerous to be outside of one's apartment because there were frequent roundups. Certain streets would be sectioned off, people's documents would be checked, and if one didn't have the right papers, one would be sent to the Umschlagplatz at once. It was also dangerous to stay at home. While home, one could hear at any given minute the ominous: "Present your documents! Come down everybody!" And then the Jewish police would make the selection in the yard: "You come with us; you may stay, you have bad papers, but if you share your money with us . . ."

Everybody knew that the salary of a Jewish policeman was meager and that he supported himself by extorting money.

I hated them. Everybody hated them. One day a policeman stopped me in the street. "Show me your documents, young man!" I pulled out my work permit. He took it away and said: "And now please take me to your apartment."

My grandpa and Lolek, who had no papers, were in the apartment! I pressed the doorbell for a long time to somehow forewarn them, but it made no sense. Where could they hide?

The policeman gathered everybody in one corner of the room and said: "Unfortunately, I have to take you all to the Umschlagplatz." He leaned out the window, whistled, and another policeman who had been a lawyer before the war and whom Aunt Marysia knew, came up, looked around, and in a vulgar tone of voice said to the first one: "Wait a minute. Perhaps there's a way to settle this."

Everything became clear to me then and there. They knew us. They came to our apartment because they were aware my senator grandfather was there and they suspected there might be some money!

I got furious. I rushed blindly to the kitchen, grabbed a knife, and wanted to assault the policeman. Mother and Aunt Marysia caught me, took away my knife. Kicked by the policeman's boot, I landed on the opposite wall. The policeman got mad. Fortunately, somehow he got placated with money. The transaction was completed. We sat down, exhausted. . . .

At long last the two were getting ready to leave. And all of a sudden, Aunt Marysia asked the policeman she knew: "Aren't you ashamed to do such things?" He replied with utmost cynicism: "I am a Marxist, ma'am. We are facing a class struggle now. My colleague who came here is a very poor man. And you, after all, are the bourgeoisie."

People hated the Germans, yet it was an abstract hatred toward a large group of uniformed soldiers, toward the Wehrmacht, the SS. It was rather rare that someone knew a German murderer personally. But the Jewish policeman was someone familiar, a man from your town, from your street, from your courtyard. He was another Jew.

They were unworthy of living. That's what I thought then and that's what I think to this day.

There was pandemonium in the streets. Every day several thousand people were rounded up. Every few minutes one could hear the screeching sound of car brakes and then the wailing of people dragged from under their beds, from closets, from nooks. Day in and day out the news reached us: this one was taken away, that one was killed.

Dead was Henryk Rozen, a high official of the Judenrat, Aunt Marysia and Uncle Marian's close friend. (Rozen went to the Umschlagplatz to save his brother, was trying to prevail on some SS soldier, but the latter wouldn't listen, pulled out his gun, and simply shot Rozen.)

Dead was little Józio Górewicz, son of a hospital employee, because when he went out onto the balcony of their apartment to stretch, unexpectedly a German from across the street killed him with a shot from his gun.

Friends from my courtyard, Leon Roland and Moniek, disappeared. They were picked up in the street. One constantly heard about someone being gone.

People started breaking down. They could not bear the stress, the hopelessness and its pervasiveness. Only I continued to live with my absurd sense of inviolability. "It has to end," I thought. "They will send away a 100,000 or a 150,000 people, and then it will end." They won't get to us.

Mother decided to bring my beloved Aunt Manya, my father's sister, and Jędruś, Aunt Dora's son, to live with us. Our apartment was safer, after all. We decided that I would be the one to bring them, since I had good papers.

"You have to bring them, otherwise they'll die!" Mother was both determined and rattled.

When I made it to Manya's place, I was shocked. She was sitting listless; she didn't want to go anywhere. "It doesn't make any sense. They will kill us anyway. They are murderers, murderers," she was saying, ready to accept whatever happened. I tried to explain, to persuade her. She had been such a level-headed person, my beloved Aunt Manya! I may have started to cry.

I don't even know how I succeeded to bring her to our apartment.

People broke down in a variety of ways. Once, a doctor we had known, Dr. Sznajderman, showed up in our apartment. He said he came to say good-bye. He had decided to go to the Umschlagplatz with his ten-year-old son.

"What are you doing, doctor?!" my mother burst out crying. "I can't take it anymore. I have no strength left to fight." He had money, documents, he was safe, but he could not tolerate the daily stress.

This Dr. Sznajderman had two sons who escaped with their mother to Złoczów at the beginning of the war. When the Germans entered Złoczów and killed their mother, they returned to Warsaw after some horrible experiences. And now the father was taking the younger one, the ten-year-old, to the Umschlagplatz and was sending the older one, the seventeen-year-old, out of the ghetto with a special group of Jewish workers (hoping that perhaps this way the boy would somehow survive).

I knew the older son. He had been in clandestine classes with Michał Dorfman. He was a very handsome boy, lanky and always very sad. There was a sort of nobility in his gaze.

One day Michał Dorfman came to see me, as usual, at the telephone exchange.

"Tomorrow I'm going with my family to the Umschlagplatz. We are starving. We have nothing left to eat."

I felt terrible. I couldn't collect my thoughts. "Michał, this means death . . ."

"We are going. It doesn't matter anymore." I wanted to cry. What could I do? How could I stop them?

"Michał! . . ." He mustn't go there! My powerlessness was unbearable. "We are starving. It doesn't matter anymore . . ." He said it calmly, without any emotion, looking straight ahead. We stood like that, facing each other.

We slept on the floor, which was disgusting and sticky from grime. In the morning, tired, we went out into the square, along with a crowd of other people as sweaty as we were.

It was hot. We were out, standing in the sun. I felt totally shattered. Next to me I saw an SS man who was keeping order in the classical pose—with a whip. "He's a 'superman'"—crossed my mind. "He's clean, immaculate. He belongs to a different world than we, the stinking humiliated mass of Jews."

The hospital employees gathered in one place. Someone on a dais read out the names of those who would be allowed to enter. I heard my name and my mother's and soon afterward the outbursts of the hospital workers because they didn't get permits. There were permits for the families of doctors and families of the administrators, and for me, too, but for the workers, many of whom had worked in the hospital for fifteen, twenty years, there were only a few "numbers." Quite upset, these workers were yelling.

I heard their shouting, stood in the scorching sun and felt only my numbing fear. Director Sztajn tried to calm people down, promising that the hospital would save them. Mother turned to me, we walked over and were led out of the gathering place in Pawia Street to the new, smaller ghetto.

I remained listless all this time and blinded by the sun. Inert, I allowed mother to lead me by the hand. We had good permits. The "cauldron" was behind us.

We were free, but I could see that the doctors were repeatedly walking over to the territory of the "cauldron." Under the pretext of taking care of official matters, they extricated hospital employees. They smuggled false "numbers" to them. There was a Dr. Flatau, who went back and forth like a mad woman. I think my mother went there as well. Somehow, in the end, the hospital workers were pulled out.

A week later, in some hospital vehicle, my mother smuggled our entire family from the cellar on Leszno Street. She got them all out in one piece; everybody survived.

Now we could organize our life in the ghetto again.

❀

6

Now, when it was over, when we survived the *Aktion* and the "cauldron," the great crisis . . . It's impossible to imagine the intensity of that fear. A thousand people every day . . . July, August, day after day, thousands of people! And now that we've survived it . . .

No, it was not a feeling of happiness. Far from it! Nothing like that. It was a kind of relaxation. Relief. Yes, we were condemned, but we had a moment of respite. We had gone through hell and now we were breathing a bit.

The ghetto was deserted. There were only about fifty to sixty thousand of us. There was no hunger, no diseases, no lice. All those who had no money or were meant to die of exhaustion had died. Those who did not secure good documents were taken away.

There were many empty apartments. It was easy to move in, take somebody's furniture or clothing. The hospital gave us a two-room apartment on Gęsia Street. Aunt Marysia and Uncle Marian found a place to live on Nalewki Street. Manya along with Jędruś moved in with her Aunt Sala. Everyday life was beginning to fall into place.

Smuggling became the main source of income for many people, and it was carefully organized. Some, that included Lolek, only carried things to a particular point within the ghetto. Others brought the things close to the wall and tossed them over. Furniture, carpets, Jewish valuables were transferred to the Aryan side. Food and cigarettes were brought into the ghetto. Those were most needed.

Smuggling was often done through the attics. People made holes in the attic walls, which separated buildings, creating passageways that sometimes connected enormous areas of the ghetto. Moving through these "canals" was safer than walking in the streets because the

Germans prowled around the ghetto and, if they saw people milling around during the day, they often fired at them. One was allowed to walk the streets of the ghetto only in the evening, after work (which was compulsory for everyone), and before the curfew. Only those who had a permit and a good reason to be there were allowed to be in the streets during the day, but the Germans often shot first and asked for permits afterward.

Rules of the game were slowly getting established in the new ghetto. A kind of stability was beginning to prevail. It was a peculiar stability because it was inseparable from a sense of threat. Every once in a while, the Germans used to engage in small *Aktionen*—they rushed in, took from two hundred up to a thousand people, and withdrew. Till the next foray. Those *Aktionen* were gradually becoming part of the normal, accepted everyday life.

Manya and Jędruś started making good money after Sala's husband found them work in the so-called Werteerfassung, the office that amassed belongings left behind by the Jews. This was an excellent job because the possessions of Jews who had been taken away could easily be stolen from the Germans. No, we didn't see anything immoral in this, although the realization that the owners might be dead was very depressing. As fate would have it, one of the first places where Manya and Jędruś went, I remember, was the hospital on Leszno Street. Unfortunately, it was too late for them to salvage any personal belongings from our apartment.

I was one of the few in the ghetto who could legally walk in the streets during the day. My mother arranged the job of delivery boy for me, and, pulling a small wagon, I transported flour, groats, and bread through the streets; I delivered sacks to hospital rooms. I wore a long frock with big blue stripes so the Germans could see that I was lawfully employed. Yet, despite the uniform, one of them might have shot me. My mother was scared for me, but there was no way out—I had to earn some money somehow. I wasn't afraid. I liked the physical effort involved in this job and the fact that I didn't have a boss. I pulled the wagon; it made a terrible din on the uneven cobblestones; the streets were deserted, ghastly; their deadliness was frightening. . . .

No, this time my life did not seem normal to me at all. I was tired. I wanted the war to end. I wanted to get out of this circle of the "plague stricken." I wanted to be able not to fear anything at long last.

The smell of burning constantly hovered over the ghetto. People used furniture pilfered from the abandoned apartments—tables, chairs, ceiling beams, anything that was wood—to heat their homes. When I walked in the streets with my wagon rumbling behind me, I could constantly sense this smell of smoldering ruins. One could feel that the end was near; that it was coming to some closure, that these were remnants of the world—a world of specters.

I had dreams of escaping somehow, of my family sending me to the Aryan side where I would find myself among friendly Poles. I could see myself walking on the well-lit streets of Warsaw, the way they were before the war. There was music, concerts in the Nardelli café, theaters.

The terror of existence is too much for me. When it presses upon me too forcefully, I start to retreat to dreams.

Once, while at home, I said childishly, "Send me to the Aryan side!" And I remember—it's a rather blurred memory—some member of the family responding: "You aren't thinking of our survival at all, are you? You're already sixteen years old and you're still so selfish!"

I actually had not thought of them. This memory has an unpleasant taste for me. It makes me aware how infantile I was then, incapable of taking responsibility for others. I had done a lot of reading and reflecting, but I was incapable of creating mature emotional ties based on responsibility. To this day I feel as if I had betrayed my family then. I had betrayed them only in my dreams. In reality, I never left them, nor did I intend to leave them. Yet, to this day I feel deeply ashamed at the thought that I wanted to leave the ghetto by myself, without them.

One day Jędruś said: "Would you like me to arrange for a permit from the Werteerfassung for you? I could do that. We would ride on motorcycles everywhere, all over the former bigger ghetto!" The prospect of riding in the bigger ghetto, of escape from the confinement of the few streets where we were presently allowed to move, was enormously tempting for me. But my mother, dead set against it, reacted: "Don't you dare!" I would have gone despite her opposition, but Jędruś preferred not to cross my mother.

Angered, instead of coming home after work, I wandered till late at night in the attics—those colossal attic tunnels—feeling furious and resentful at my mother. I walked across those fractured walls of buildings and I imagined with satisfaction how worried they were at home.

At that time I was already beginning to distance myself from my family. I looked critically at all of them. All kinds of old and new occurrences were accumulating in my memory: the image of Uncle Marian, still before the "Big *Aktion*," giving Grandma a large sum of money (he could have come by that money only by taking bribes; he worked in the Jewish Council assigning people to forced labor, and it was well known that anyone could avoid forced labor by paying a bribe). I also remember a woman, Grandma's relative, who, still in the starvation-ridden old ghetto, would come to us crying and pleading for money (at that time, money was a matter of life or death). Grandma would give her something, but once, after the woman had left, Grandma said: "She's young and beautiful, couldn't she support herself some other way?" (Of course, Grandma had prostitution in mind.) The woman never came back.

One of my worst memories goes back to the times before the "Big *Aktion*," when Grandpa and Lolek had just come back from the east, and we were just running out of supplies. The family decided that Grandpa, as a prominent personage before the war, would discreetly appeal for help to the Jewish Council. That was done. The council picked from the minor merchants in the ghetto an owner of a small wholesale needle business and ordered him to pay a percentage of his profits to our family.

That was blackmail! That was outright robbery! And it was being done by my own family, which had a tradition of integrity, which raised me with the myth of my father as an honest and uncompromising man. The wholesaler couldn't defend himself because all merchants in the ghetto—including him—functioned in violation of the prevailing regulations, so the Judenrat could destroy him at any moment. The thought that my relatives could rob someone so ruthlessly was difficult for me to bear.

Earlier, in similar circumstances, I had protested. I remember that before the ghetto was established, when my mother mercilessly fought for her position at the hospital, I told her several times that from the ethical point of view I didn't like it. But she would reply with such indignation that the whole family was doing what it could to survive and all I did was criticize—that eventually I learned to keep quiet, especially since I ate their food and benefited from their dishonestly obtained goods.

The arrangement with the wholesaler lasted till the end of the ghetto. He survived the "Big *Aktion;*" so did we—and we continued to live off his earnings. Every month Lolek checked the man's bookkeeping to make sure he wasn't "cheating us." And talking about that "cheating," Lolek would always make a sly face.

One day Lolek was checking the books at the wholesaler's apartment, when suddenly one of the little *Aktionen* began, and the Germans, for some unknown reason, pounded on the door.

Lolek had no documents on him. Had they caught him, it would have meant his end, so he crawled under the bed. The Germans charged in, dispersed all over the apartment, arrested everybody who was home, but did not look under the bed. One of the women living in the apartment left the house barefoot because she knew that had she looked for her shoes under the bed, the Germans would have discovered Lolek.

An hour later everything calmed down. Lolek felt terribly hungry (it was a nervous reaction). He came out from under the bed and began prowling the kitchen. He devoured everything in sight. Suddenly, it occurred to him: "They won't be back!"—and he started searching the apartment. He took the entire supply of needles and returned home.

Shortly afterward, the wholesaler and his family were let go (they had good papers, it seems), and the wholesaler came to us pleading for the return of the needles because without them, he would be totally ruined. In reply the family said to him: "We need to confer before we return them." And they ordered him to go home.

I don't know what happened next. I have probably blocked it from my memory. A total blank. A white blot in my head. I think they returned them. It's hard for me to think about it.

I kept reading a lot: *Buddenbrooks* by Mann, Dostoyevsky's *Demons,* Żeromski's *Early Spring.* I read whatever fell into my hands. Once, Jędruś brought me to the Werteerfassung book warehouse. It was a colossal book collection. "Take whatever books you want!" he said. And I did.

Often I looted books in abandoned apartments. I found Spinoza's *Ethics* and a crystallography textbook. I studied logic, philosophy, math. On my own, of course. No one contemplated underground schooling then. We were living on borrowed time. And to organize schooling would have been absurd.

Ludwik Asz and his mother lived in our apartment building. So did a young doctor who played the piano, and a violinist, a German Jew, a former student of Aunt Manya's (she taught him English). Those two played classical music duets in the evenings. Their playing turned into a kind of concert series for the neighbors. I would come, Ludwik, another neighbor, a Mr. Wilk, and we listened to Mozart. I remember those evenings. It would get dark outdoors; the curfew was on; one couldn't go anywhere; and they played and played.

Sometimes Ludwik, his mother, and I would conjure up spirits. We would switch on a little night lamp in a corner, put our hands over a round table, place a plate with letters and an arrow drawn on it on the table, and hold our hands above it. Usually, a moment came when the plate would start turning and the arrow, pointing to the letters, would give us an answer. We once asked when the war would be over. On February 20—the plate responded.

❋

7

In January, without any warning, the Germans entered the ghetto in large force. In a matter of a few days, they took away four to five thousand people.

This was a reminder. We were breathing with relief after the "Big *Aktion*," we were resting, and they let us know that the sentence was in. We just had to wait for it to be carried out. Also, that there was still some time. One could do something. One could save oneself.

At that time in response to the order "Present your documents! Come down everybody!" nobody came down. Whoever could hid in a cellar or an attic. The Germans, along with the Jewish policemen, broke into apartments and dragged people out. The horror returned, this time for good.

We hid in the attic. Again I was paralyzed by a psychotic fear. Everything around me seemed bizarre and foreign. I was afraid I would lose myself, that in a moment I would not be myself. Next to me sat a girl who for some unknown reason disgusted me. I was possessed by an obsessive thought that any moment I would turn into someone as repulsive as she was.

It was terribly cold in the attic. The wind was howling; sand was blowing in through the cracks in the roof. We cuddled up because of the cold. The Germans used to enter the ghetto in the morning, conduct the *Aktion*, then always leave in the evening, and the next day start all over again. When they left the ghetto at nightfall, we would go down to the apartment to warm up and cook something.

One day Grandpa and Grandma went down too early. They didn't realize the Germans were still in the ghetto. Suddenly, they were startled by loud steps in the stairwell and pounding on the door. They didn't know what to do. Fortunately, our maid Regina, a big Jewish woman with red hair and enormous fishlike eyes (I couldn't stand her), happened to be with them. She shoved my grandparents behind a wardrobe where there was some hole in the wall. She pushed the wardrobe against the wall, so they couldn't be seen, and at the last moment she barely had time enough to hide in a coal bin in the hall. The bin wasn't very big and Regina was enormous. A Jewish police-man lifted the cover. She shot a glance at him with that fishlike eye of hers . . . No, nothing happened. The policeman looked at Regina for a while and closed the cover. The Germans left. Thanks to Regina, a big, disheveled Jewish woman with a hefty rump, Grandpa and Grandma were saved.

Regina was my grandmother's friend of sorts. Despite the class dif-ference, they constantly debated issues in Yiddish. They would sit next to each other in the kitchen. Regina addressed my grandmother as "Madame," and Grandma used to say "would Regina" do this or that.

I couldn't stand Regina. I found her physically repulsive. To this day I think with much pain how unjust that was.

We spent four days in the attic. On the fifth day the Germans didn't enter the ghetto; the *Aktion* was over. People went to work again. The black market started again; ordinary life resumed. Everything seemed to have returned to normal, but any day then we expected the final ex-termination. We knew we were very close to it. Any moment the Ger-mans would come and liquidate us.

People in the ghetto were hastily preparing hiding places—in at-tics, in cellars. Whoever had money built special shelters. Grandpa took it upon himself to organize the construction of a shelter for many people (an undertaking with grand flair); he collected funds for the timber and expert workers, persuaded people to help with the con-struction. I helped, too. I dug dirt, carried sacks. All of us felt the end was at hand, and yet we harbored some hope.

The hope was that maybe the war would be over before the Germans managed to destroy the ghetto. Everybody dreamed about that. After all, the Germans had been defeated at Stalingrad, were chased away from Rostov and Kharkov. One day I heard cannon shots (these were German antiaircraft exercises), and I thought, deceiving myself, of course: "Perhaps these are Russians. It's possible they broke through the front that fast! Don't the German communiqués lie constantly . . ."

Once, after another German defeat, I met a doctor I knew from the hospital, Dr. Rattner, in the street. Overjoyed, he grabbed me by the arm and said:" Do you see? Do you see how the Krauts are getting kicked in the ass?"

At one point the rumor spread that if one had the citizenship of a Latin American country, one could be saved, because the Germans would send him to a transitional camp in Vittel in Alsace, and then to South America. This was all turned on its head—who in Poland could have had the citizenship of a Latin American country? And why would the Germans save such people? But people were clutching at straws.

They attempted to obtain such documents, to buy them. So did we. At that time, my grandfather used to have a visitor, his young protégé, Hilel Zajdman, a journalist affiliated before the war with the Agudat Israel Party, who promised to procure the citizenship. He said: "You'll get it any day now." In the end he himself left. He was one of the few who escaped from the camp in Vittel and were saved. All of that was, of course, another German provocation.

A colossal number of people were thinking then of escaping from the ghetto. Earlier, before the "Big *Aktion,*" only those who had Polish friends and safe hiding places on the Aryan side escaped. At this point some were opting for the most risky move: money in exchange for hiding. A hiding place in exchange for payment was something very uncertain. What would people who hid you for profit do when your resources ended? Would they throw you into the street then? Or would they rob you at once and take you to the police? One heard about incidents of that sort all the time. Those who managed to save their lives in the nick of time by escaping from *szmalcowniks* came back to the ghetto repeatedly.

Despite all that, the Jews were determined. More and more of them left the ghetto. Uncle Marian's sister and her husband—very Jewish looking, with heavy Jewish accents, but with lots of money—decided to go to the Aryan side. We, too, through Uncle Marian's good offices, made a certain move. We entrusted my little four-year-old cousin Rysia into the hands of a friendly policeman, whom Marian, as a lawyer, knew from before the war. The policeman was given money and was to receive a big reward after the war.

My family also considered sending me away. My mother even telephoned Mr. Skoczek, my father's old and closest coworker, who was very attached to our family, but the Skoczeks refused. (They were already hiding some Jewish girl, and, on top of that, at the Wola district hospital, they were heavily involved in underground activities on behalf of the Home Army). Mother also called, though without much expectation, Mr. Stefan, our prewar Polish hairdresser. To our surprise, Mr. Stefan immediately responded: "I'll take him. Of course, I'll take him." And it was clear that he would do it, and not for money.

This was an opportunity. Mr. Stefan was almost like a family friend. He was a simple, uneducated, exceptionally cordial man. When before the war he used to come to cut our hair, it was like a holiday for me. I would sit in front of the mirror; he put a white frock on me, walked around me with scissors and a razor; and all the time he would tell me about his 1905 adventures. I listened to his stories as if they were fairy tales. He didn't hesitate for a moment to take me in.

I could have left. I could have saved myself. I could have stayed with someone in whom all of us had confidence, but Mother said then: "No, you won't make it!" What's interesting, I didn't feel hurt by that at all. Now that I could have left, somehow the Aryan side didn't attract me. I understood (basically, I understood all along) that it was not the Nardelli café that awaited me there but fear. Repeated escapes and fear. And separation.

"You won't go. You won't make it!" Most likely, Mother didn't want to be separated from me, either.

Leaflets of the Jewish Fighting Organization could be seen more and more often. Underground newspapers were passed from hand to hand; information was conveyed: again some vile Jewish policeman was killed; again some Jewish financial potentate was abducted so money to purchase weapons could be extorted from him. News spread instantly, like lightning. I would swell with pride on hearing about the successive coups. After each such occurrence, I went out and, while passing a Jewish policeman in the street, I peered at him ominously. I straightened up and peered, convinced that now it was he who had to be terribly afraid.

Perhaps, if I hadn't been my mother's son, I would have attempted to join the Jewish Fighting Organization. But escape from her over-protective clutches was totally impossible for me. All that was left to me was the daily wait for another traitor to be killed, and yet another! Had I possessed a gun, I would have murdered Jewish policemen and even tortured them! My hatred toward them was simply eating me up.

Everybody around me was glad that there was a resistance movement in the ghetto. And I don't know of anyone who was scandalized by the fact that the Jewish Fighting Organization was kidnapping rich Jews. Even my grandfather—with all his bourgeois mentality—accepted it, was pleased. Of course, no one was of the opinion that the resistance would spare us from death. Yet we had the feeling that it bestowed on us a kind of dignity. This time it would be different. Unlike those before us, we would not go to the Umschlagplatz willingly. Yes, the end would come but not quite according to Hitler's scenario.

In the evening the family used to gather and listen to Grandpa read his memoirs. He wrote them in Yiddish with the intention of publishing them later on. Everybody listened and then analyzed the text. I was the only one who kept silent. I couldn't discuss the contents of the memoirs because I didn't understand Yiddish.

I remember them saying how important it would be after the war to have the memoirs published and how much money it would bring. On the one hand, they expected the liquidation of the ghetto perhaps the next day; on the other—they made plans for long after the war.

This duality of thinking was a frequent phenomenon in the ghetto. I remember this. My grandfather owned a house on Nalewki Street. In it, there was a bakery managed by the baker Kahane. That Kahane was negotiating with Grandpa. In exchange for the two or three loaves of bread he gave us free of charge every day (this was the cheapest bread, made of potato skins; horrible, but in those days we liked it very much), after the war he would not pay my grandfather any rent. Kahane wanted this arrangement to be lifelong, but Grandpa didn't agree. They settled upon a five-year deal.

I still remember how that baker's son, who happened to be Lolek's classmate, laughed at their absurd negotiations. "None of us will survive this war! What are they arguing about?" But the thought processes in such situations are often complicated. "It's true, we don't know what will happen in a month or two," Grandpa probably thought, "but if we do survive, why shouldn't he pay me rent?"

The family's total attention was directed now to the matter of survival. And what else could be done. I was enlisted to help Lolek smuggle. Mother didn't want me to do it, but Lolek coerced her: "I am risking my life; have you thought of that?!"

I ran through the attics with him, carried things. It didn't frighten me. My eyes were sharp, my body nimble. I was convinced that I would sense the danger in time and manage to escape.

I willingly completed the various tasks imposed on me by the family. But I never initiated anything. Even if I had wanted to, I probably couldn't have come up with anything and propose it. I was not practical. And I felt that was the reason my family almost totally stopped paying attention to me.

Earlier, there was room in my family for emotions directed toward children. Now, that energy was exhausted. Only enough was left for indispensable efforts.

I hardly spoke to my mother, although we slept in the same bed (the apartment was cramped). She came home from the hospital very late, exhausted. . . .

As to family deliberations—how to obtain bread, how to obtain money—I could only listen to them.

One day I insulted my grandmother terribly. I told her she was stupid, uneducated. Later, I was ashamed. How could I have attacked this woman—good to me, warm and caring—so thoughtlessly?!

I constantly walked about anxious and irritated. I had no other community but my family, yet I sensed a growing distance between us. I was beginning to feel truly frightened! I had the impression that little by little I was ceasing to belong. That was horrible; that seemed to me more threatening than death. What it meant to me was total loneliness, existential loneliness. I was not afraid of the Germans. I was not afraid of the end of the ghetto, but I was afraid of just that, of the isolation from my family.

One day I managed to see Marian Lewenfisz. I found out that he and his parents were staying in Schultz's workshop in a part of the ghetto separated from us by several closed streets. (People employed in sev-

In August or September, the Germans announced that the area of the ghetto would be reduced and that old documents would no longer entitle one to live there. New documents would be required, and one would be able to obtain them at a special place where all inhabitants of the ghetto were to report. If one would go there with one's lawful employer and the entire group of his employees, one might get a permit (called "a number"), but then again—one might not, because employers would receive a limited number of "numbers" and there would not be enough for everybody. Those who received a "number" would live within the significantly reduced territory of the ghetto. Those who did not get a "number" would be taken away. Leszno Street, where our hospital was located, would be excluded from the ghetto.

To go or not to go? This was now a gamble for one's life. The family decided that we would not go. My mother alone would go, since given the rigid criteria, only she had a chance to obtain a legal document. We would hide in the cellar of our apartment building, and when the "*kociot,*" the "cauldron" (that's how the latest operation was commonly referred to), was over, somehow mother would get us out.

We went down. The cellar was enormous. Our entire family hid there and a lot of other people affiliated with the hospital. We were sitting, not knowing what would happen that day or the next, nor how long we would have to stay in the cellar.

It was exactly then that I was seized by a terrible fear. I fell into an unbearable psychotic state. I comprehended nothing, sat petrified as if I were hallucinating. All familiar objects appeared foreign and threatening to me.

I am capable of retaining a sense of normalcy in an abnormal world for a long time. It is enough for me to have some fairly familiar background, my family, a regular routine. But when that background disappears, my equilibrium breaks down acutely. In the cellar of my apartment building, I felt totally devastated.

Two days later my mother's assistant showed up and said that the director of the hospital, Sztajn, had obtained a permit for me.

That was liberation. I could go out! I'd see daylight! The fear was gone instantly. I was myself again.

I managed to find my mother somewhere on Franciszkańska Street, I believe. The night was approaching. We were herded into some school.

eral small factories, called workshops, remained in the large ghetto and lived in them, as if stranded on islands, cut off from the world.) I kept trying to join some people who were being taken to the large ghetto to work. Finally, I succeeded to reach the Lewenfiszes.

They were very happy to see me. They invited me to supper and even wanted me to stay for the night. Marian, brilliant and arrogant as usual, was bragging about the books he had managed to loot. I bragged about my books. It was growing dark. I had to return home.

Jędruś told me that Stefan was in one of the workshops. He had conveyed his regards through Jędruś. I never saw Stefan again.

I was alone. Ludwik no longer lived in our apartment house. He and his mother crossed to the Aryan side. The only peer with whom I had contact was Jędruś. I visited him; he told me what he was doing, how he lived. We had always liked each other—Jędruś, Dora's son, and I. He was an intelligent, vivacious, and cheerful boy, but now he grew manly, taller than me (though he was a year younger), broad-shouldered, and very independent.

Jędruś had started following his own bizarre path a long time ago. Even before the "Big *Aktion*" when Grandpa from Kiliński Street and Dora were still alive, he dropped by the house one day in the uniform of the "13." Grandpa and Dora almost fainted from the shock. People from the "13," the official Jewish organization created to control the underground economic activities of the ghetto, were despised, because the "13" unquestionably collaborated with the Germans and attracted lots of blackmailers and bribe takers. Jędruś certainly had nothing to do with the "13"—he could not have, he was too young—and he had either stolen the uniform or received it as a gift. But we were horrified and astounded. We couldn't understand why the uniform impressed him so much.

An interesting thing happened to Jędruś. Obviously antagonistic toward the Germans, he nevertheless absorbed some of their values. He liked power, the SS whip, the stick; he savored sharp German propaganda slogans. In a novel he had once begun to write (it was supposed to have been a novel about him and me; my name in the novel was Christopher), words like *judenrein* (free of Jews) or *Ausrottung* (pulling out with the roots) appeared quite frequently. Jędruś knew, of course—he was too smart not to have known—that he himself was one of those whom the words *judenrein* and *Ausrottung* concerned, but at the same time one could see that uttering these words and listening to their sound brought him particular pleasure.

These strange psychological processes appeared in many young people in the ghetto, particularly those who—like Jędruś later on at Werteerfassung—worked alongside the Germans. During that collaboration, social ties and even friendships developed. I remember walking with Jędruś in the street once, when a fellow waved at him and said: "Hello, Jędruś!" "Hello, Jaś," Jędruś replied. "Who was it?" I asked because I was intrigued that they greeted each other like friends. "Oh, it's an SS man I know, but in plain clothes."

He lived in a world totally different from mine.

In the last weeks of the ghetto, Jędruś joined a group of youths who lived life with great intensity. They danced, drank a lot, made love, lived it up greedily. Every dawn could have brought the end. It would be the end of life, but today we were still alive.

It's interesting that at those parties of theirs—so I was told by Jędruś—occasionally SS men appeared as acquaintances of the young people. They socialized with the Jewish youths. They were a part of the world getting ready to die.

How could I live then, knowing that I would soon die? I don't know. I can't answer the question. I read books; I walked around the ghetto as usual. I remember distinctly what I read, but I don't remember what I thought, what I did, what I talked about. It's horrifying how little I remember of those days! When I talk about the years after the war, I can open up, talk about many events. But the war period remains murky in my mind. A bit like a dream. Something is missing there. The riches of memory are missing.

I remember merely summaries, what I have summarized during my life, the history I told myself in my lifetime.

I don't remember the apartment in which Jędruś and Manya had lived. I have some kind of a gap. Why don't I remember a thing?

Well, I do remember a few incidents. For instance, I was standing near Muranowski Square (today that's Muranowski Street) and saw that Poles brought from the outside were working there. I knew their work would end soon and they would go back to the Aryan side, and I envied them terribly.

Or I met a musician I knew in the street. He asked me "Do you know Rachmaninoff's concerts?" and began to sing. And he said: "Oh, what wonderful concerts they are!"

Or I met the hospital bookkeeper's son. He was a bit older than me, supposedly very intelligent, but we hadn't had the opportunity to talk at length. We started talking. We were shy. All around us was the terrible stench of the ruins. We were both self-conscious. He had such a sensitive, dark face. I wanted the conversation to last forever, for him to become my friend. Such a shy overture among the stench of the ruins was playing out between us . . .

✿

8

Passover arrived, the Jewish Easter. Grandpa insisted that we should have matzo at home during those days. I was the one to deliver it through the attics. Somewhere in those attics I jumped ineptly and broke a leg. My mother was despondent.

"Don't worry!" the doctor in the hospital appeased her. "In a few weeks we'll take the cast off and he'll be running around again."

Two days later, on April 19, the ghetto uprising broke out.

The Germans and the Ukrainians entered the ghetto. Mother was beside herself, mainly because of my leg.

We ran off to the attic, the same one we had stayed in during the January *Aktion*. That was our only hiding place (money ran out for completion of the shelter built under my grandfather's supervision). The attic was walled up, concealed; one could enter it only by removing a few bricks and crawling through the opening.

It was a beautiful late April spring. The sky could be seen through cracks in the roof; one could feel the warm wind. Along with us, neighbors from our stairwell and employees of the hospital were hiding in the attic. We heard shooting all the time—machine guns from the German side and solitary shots from the Jewish. "Oh, if only we had weapons and could shoot at them!" a hospital worker exclaimed excitedly.

The stench of burning was reaching us. The Germans dragged people out of their houses and then burned the houses, methodically, house after house. One day we saw Polish firemen on our roof, attempting to control the spread of fire. We were petrified. They were not our primary threat, but we didn't want them to see us.

Once—perhaps on the third or fourth day—I fell asleep sitting up in the attic. I was tired. Suddenly, something woke me up. I opened my eyes, moved a bit. Mother grabbed my arm and put her finger on her lips to silence me. I looked around and noticed how tense everybody was. No one said a word. I understood that something was going on.

At one point I heard a loud *ein, zwei, drei* (one, two, three) behind the wall, then a pistol shot. Somebody was removing the loose bricks from the outside. It was a Jewish policeman. We had been discovered.

I looked at my mother. The hole in the wall was narrow, so no one from the outside entered it. But I knew for sure that we would have to crawl through the hole very soon. "Stay, if you wish," my mother said. I understood. With my leg in a cast, I could be shot. "Will you stay with me?" I asked her. "No, I'll go with the family," she answered. "Then I'm going with you," I responded.

We crawled out one by one. It was funny: a few Jewish policemen, one German, and a whole bunch of us. We could have just killed that German! We were coming down. Half a flight down, I saw Dr. Rattner. He suddenly opened some door leading to the hospital and escaped. A few people followed him. The German didn't react. No one chased them. I could have escaped as well.

We were led, egged on. I had a feeling of absolute unreality. For so long it hadn't happened to me; for so long I believed it wouldn't happen to me! And now reality had caught up with me. I was walking the same path as thousands of others. Umschlagplatz, transport to Treblinka, and gassing awaited me any moment.

I hobbled along. We walked on Gęsia Street, then turned right somewhere. The ghetto was in flames. I hobbled along. I was terribly afraid. Supported on one side by my mother, by Lolek on the other, I limped along. I hopped on one leg. Grandpa walked behind me, saying to me softly (that was totally unlike him): " Don't be afraid, child. Don't be afraid. Hold out a bit longer."

I concentrated with all my strength to make it to the Umschlagplatz with them. We all knew that if I had stopped for a moment, the Germans would have shot me.

We were crammed into the school at Umschlagplatz. The classrooms, the corridors were terribly crowded. People were milling about everywhere; they were in shock. We met people we knew: Dr. Rattner (they caught him, after all); Nacia, my mother's cheerful cousin (I remember how well she imitated and mocked the Orthodox Jews from Grandpa's party; she considered them hypocrites); Maryś Eierweiss, my kindergarten classmate.

Maryś and I tried to get to the attic, but an armed SS man was in our way. He stood on the stairs. We turned back. On the staircase I found a Jewish policeman's ID. I examined it and hesitated. I wandered if I could use the ID to get out. Suddenly, some hysterical woman grabbed my elbow: "He was my friend! They killed him! I won't let you escape with the ID!"

We stayed at the school. Another day, night, and yet another day went by. From those days I remember only these scenes. An SS man walked into one of the classrooms; a woman holding a few-months-old baby was sitting against the wall; the SS man took the child from her and started talking to the baby gently in German. He gave the child back to her.

Lolek was talking to my mother. He was telling her about the woman in the ghetto he got involved with. I knew her. She was attractive, a bit harsh, but nice. Lolek was saying how much he cared about her but that Grandpa was opposed to their relationship.

The Ukrainians entered into the classroom to prowl. Grandpa pushed my grandmother's ring and the gold eyeglasses frame inside the cast on my leg. The Ukrainians grabbed Grandma and pulled her earrings, her jewelry out of her purse. She didn't react. She was in a state of total shock. Grandpa said to them: "Leave the poor woman alone," and then one of the Ukrainians whacked him on the head with the butt of his gun.

Execution of the Judenrat was taking place in the school yard. We watched it from our windows. They killed several top executives of the council. Among them were Lichtenbaum, Wielikowski, and others. My Aunt Marysia said: "That means they are ending the ghetto; that's their last *Aktion* in the ghetto."

One day we noticed Aunt Manya standing on the other side of Stawki Street. She was free. Her street hadn't been "combed" yet. Manya stood there, looking at our windows. We waved at her; she saw us but just spread her hands in helplessness. She lifted them in a despairing gesture over her head. We understood. There was nothing she could do but show us her gesture. That was a kind of farewell.

At one point I asked my mother if there was any chance for our survival. "Alas, no. All of us have to die," Mother said in a quiet, authoritative voice.

I calmed down. I received the news as if I were accepting death. I started talking to my mother. I told her that I was probably a bad son. I told her that sincerely, from my heart, as if it were my last confession. "No, it wasn't so," Mother appeased me and consoled me.

I was no longer afraid. Nor was I rebellious. I began contemplating, however, what death would be like. I tried to imagine it, to talk about it with someone, to share it with someone, but I couldn't express anything. I had a need for some kind of loftiness, but whatever I wanted to say seemed stupid and trivial to me. So finally I gave up.

We were sitting. Suddenly, the Ukrainians charged in and took four people closest to the door out to the school yard. We heard the shots. They killed them. Now, among the four sitting closest to the door were Marian and Grandpa. We contemplated moving to another classroom, but Grandpa said: "What's the difference. It's ending anyway."

The Ukrainians took them to the yard. I was sitting, convinced that these were the last moments of my life. We heard shots. A moment later Grandpa returned pale as chalk. "Where is Marian?" Marysia asked. "Marian is no more. He was shot."

What had occurred was that all four were asked to dig a shallow grave. Then they shot the remaining three but not Grandpa. Why? Nobody knows. "He died praying," Grandpa said about Marian. "He started *Shma Israel* and then they killed him."

Marysia cried. Mother embraced her to calm her. "Maybe I should have divorced Marian," Marysia suddenly burst out crying. "I know he had terrible shortcomings, but despite them I still loved him." Marian, disliked by my family, probably married Marysia for her dowry, but she, intelligent, supportive, helped him out, and their marriage seemed to be good.

"Maybe I should have divorced him." Marysia kept crying, now curled up. It surprised me. I didn't understand it

Every day new people were crammed into the school. We were waiting for the transport.

A few days later the train arrived. We were chased out into the square. We started walking. People said: "The cars are here; they're loading," but somehow I saw nothing. We were walking slowly. I was stuck, immobilized by the mob moving step by step. Mother and Aunt Ala (the wife of one of my uncles) were ahead of me. Next to me was Aunt Marysia. We were walking next to the fence that separated the Umschlagplatz from the ghetto. Suddenly, I noticed a hole in the fence and behind the fence an empty street. "That's impossible"— crossed my mind. "If I only try, they'll shoot me at once!"

I looked around. There were no guards. I made an instantaneous decision. I didn't ask Mother nor anyone else. I just bolted and crawled through. Aunt Marysia followed me at once. And Mother. And Aunt Ala. And a man with a bandaged head.

We ran. The fellow with the bandage on his head yelled: "Go left; I know a shelter out there to the left!" We ran. I dragged my broken leg. We rushed into some house. I turned around and I saw just Aunt Marysia and that fellow. Mother and Ala were gone. Marysia had seen them turn right, toward the building that housed Werteerfassung.

We went down to the cellar. The man with the bandaged head began pounding on the door: "Let us in! Let us in!" They didn't open. "Let us in!"

Finally, they let us in. It was totally dark there. We groped around to find some place to lie down. We were saved.

"Could it be providence that you and I succeeded in saving our lives?" Aunt Marysia wondered. And immediately afterward, she said: "Promise me that if we survive, you'll never part from me. You have been like a son to me. I had no children and I have loved you like a son." I promised. I loved her very much, too.

We stayed in the shelter. Next to us was a strange couple who spoke German to each other. He was a Polish Jew; she was a German, only one-quarter Jewish. She could have left the ghetto but wanted to share his fate. We and that couple formed a separate group.

Hours, days went by. To us the shelter was like a grave. I was terribly hungry. People had some food supplies but were unwilling to give us anything, not even flour, except for drinking water. I realized I wasn't saved at all. I wanted to leave, but my aunt wouldn't. We were in danger of starvation, I tried to persuade her. If we left the shelter, we could hide in some apartment, ferret out some food, and then run off somewhere else.

But my aunt didn't want to. She was afraid. We stayed.

It was in the morning. People started yelling that the house was on fire. I could feel the smoke and the heat. "We have to leave! Otherwise, we'll die!" Everything was happening in the flash of lightning. We left. Ukrainians were waiting for us outside.

They chased us into a train right away. We didn't even cross the Umschlagplatz. A Ukrainian noticed my cast. He approached me, wanted to pull me out and kill me. But we were very close to the train. Marysia helped me, pushed me in so I could get my legs inside as fast as possible. Someone extended a hand from the inside to pull me in. I struggled to get in. One more effort, one more and I was inside the car. Saved again. A moment later Marysia stood beside me.

❁

9

We were standing. There were probably about 150 of us in the car. There is no way to imagine the huddling and congestion! A tiny window was located at the very top of the car. Only those close to it could breathe.

The train took off. It moved a little and stopped again. We didn't budge the whole night. People were fainting; some died. Poles with bottles of water were swarming around the car. They were asking twenty, thirty dollars (yes, dollars!) for passing a bottle through the little barred window.

At last, we were actually moving. The question arose: were we going to Treblinka or somewhere else. Treblinka meant instant death, but people standing next to the window said we were going southeast. That implied Majdanek, Lublin, which also meant death, but perhaps not right away.

Some wanted to escape. There were two ways to do it: you either had to remove a board in the floor and lower yourself onto the tracks so the train would pass above you, or you had to jump out the window. I would not have had the courage to lower myself; that's a horrifying thing, but I would have jumped out the window despite my broken leg. Marysia would have done it, too. There were even people on the train who had files (one could always find strong people who knew how to do things), but others said that if the Ukrainians saw us jump, they would start shooting. No one was allowed to approach the window. Nobody jumped.

We reached Majdanek the next day. There were rumors that, for money, Polish railroad workers were willing to hide someone and bring him back to Warsaw. We attempted to negotiate with a railroad employee, but he was afraid. We got out of the car. No Germans awaited us on the ramp, only Jews with horsewhips. They were brutal. They yelled "son of a bitch" at everybody. One could tell by their accents that they were from the eastern territories of Poland.

We were herded into a big square. Several thousand people were swarming there. They were all in a state of shock, moving around, forming some groups, new little groups, looking here and there watchfully—perhaps something else could be done. Perhaps there was still a way to save oneself.

Marysia vanished from my eyes. She came back an hour later; said she met Grandpa, who had already been there for a week. He had a towel and was on his way to a shower. "For sixty plus years I have been a VIP and today I live like a beggar," he told her. "But one has to accept it. Such are the fortunes of men." Marysia cried.

Suddenly, I met our maid Regina. She was overjoyed to find us alive because she had thought we were already dead.

There was a commotion. The Germans, who stood on an elevation separated from us, ordered us to assemble and start walking somewhere. "Don't budge!" Regina yelled suddenly. I could see she was flying into a rage. "If they are to kill us, let them kill us here!" The spirit of a folk hero seemed to have entered her. She was ready to lead people in an uprising!

Marysia responded to that in a strange way: "No, we have to trust the Germans now. So far, we have resisted them, but now is the time to trust them." I listened to these words incredulously. Were they uttered by Marysia, who all along had been insisting that the Germans wanted to hoodwink us at any cost, to cheat us, to disarm us psychologically?

Unexpectedly, I met Dr. Wdowiński, my father's friend. I was glad. We stood next to each other. Wdowiński told me he had seen Jędruś, who—when the Germans were looking for doctors—exclaimed "I'm a doctor!" A German holding a whip allegedly looked at him gently and remarked "You're too young" (Jędruś was fifteen), but Jędruś replied: "That's true, but I'm an orderly." He joined the doctors and was most likely taken to the camp in Trawniki.

They were segregating us. We were standing, Wdowiński and I, among a group of men. Marysia was already taken away from me. "Line up by eight and walk!" the Jewish "capos" yelled. We started marching. I passed a German with a dog whip. He noticed the cast on my leg and yelled: "Du, du raus!" and pointed to a group consisting of women and people unfit to work.

I joined the group. Marysia was there. She grabbed me and said: "Try again; enter the line of men in the middle. Maybe you'll make it!" She knew her group would be killed, and so she pushed me in to save my life.

I tried again and succeeded. I passed the German with a whip without him noticing me. I walked by Marysia. Marysia stayed behind.

We were herded into a train. I stood next to Wdowiński. Again, the nightmare of the train ride. Again, there was no air to breathe.

The train stopped on the second day. It was in the Budzyń camp. The German commander of the camp—Lagerfuehrer Feiks, handsome, blond—lectured us from the very moment we entered: "For possession of money—death! For an attempt to escape—death!" For this, for that—death. And on and on he went. It was a whole litany.

"And now"—Feiks continued—"you must put down all your valuables." For me this was the first decision I had to make on my own: should I give up Grandma's ring and gold eyeglasses frame or not.

People were throwing their money and jewelry in a pile. There was more and more of it. I didn't move. "Is that all?" Feiks asked when the agitation finally died down. He called someone out of a line and began searching. He found some money. He shot the man dead on the spot.

"You still have a chance. Give up your money," he said. More people threw their money. And some more. The pile of valuables was growing higher and higher. I didn't budge. I had made a decision.

Finally, the search ended. Now the German started walking among the rows. He was assisted by the chief of the Jewish administration of the camp, a tall and terribly skinny man. I noticed to my surprise that he was wearing a Polish military uniform.

They stopped next to me. *Lagerfuehrer* Feiks looked at my cast, frowned, and said something in German. I didn't understand it, but I knew I was in trouble. The German told the Jew to translate. "Your leg. That's merely a twisted ankle, right? the Jewish commander asked me in Polish. He looked at me sternly, intelligently, and I realized at once that he was prompting me how to reply. "Yes, merely a twisted ankle," I dutifully repeated after him. "And the cast will be removed in a few days, right?" he continued to prompt me gravely. "Yes, in a few days," I replied hastily. He translated it. The German commander looked at me with hesitation. Finally, he waved me away and left. He did not shoot me. Thanks to the chief of the Jewish administration he did not shoot me.

They led us into the camp. It was surrounded by a double barbed wire. Guard towers were positioned at the corners. The guards were Ukrainians. Their club was outside the gate; that's where they rested.

The first thing they did was to line us up in rows. They painted big red crosses on the backs of our clothes. Now one couldn't escape anywhere. Then we went to the barrack. It was dark, long, with bunks for two in three tiers. About three hundred people slept there.

I lay down in the bunk I was sharing with Wdowiński. I was ashamed: I had lice. I didn't tell Wdowiński. Perhaps he had lice, too, and didn't tell me. . . . In the morning I felt moisture in my pants. I had wet my bed for the first time since my childhood. I stank. That was terrible. I had no change of clothing. The stinking clothes were drying on me.

After roll call we were taken to bathe. I washed myself for the first time since April 18. I soaped myself up with a tiny cake of soap. Strong, tall men were milling all around me. And suddenly, I started thinking of myself in a way I had not thought of myself before: "I'm small. I'm rather weak. I have a baby face. I won't make it." I looked at the strong men and sensed a terrible feeling of contempt for myself.

As we were leaving the bathroom, someone yelled: "They are distributing straw mattresses!" People ran ahead, pulled at the mattresses; everybody wanted to choose the best for himself. I stood aside, helpless, and I got the worst mattress with rotten straw. I had a hard time carrying it, too. Humiliated, I struggled and pulled and held myself in contempt! Such contempt is a feeling a hundred times worse than fear.

For the first three weeks, I had this absurd feeling that soon I would return to the apartment in the Czyste neighborhood, to my family. Mother, Grandma, and Grandpa would be there; everything would be just like before the war. It was not a dream or a vision but a kind of strange presence of the prewar world in me. During the moments when I clearly realized what the reality was, I panicked. And it was only when somehow the sense of the presence of my family returned to me that I could go on living.

I was constantly sleepy. While, from the moment we were captured in the ghetto, my attention had been strained, vigilant to the limits of impossibility, now it was totally blunted. I responded to life in the camp by sleepiness. I was behind barbed wires, plucked not only out of my family but out of my entire former milieu. I lived among several thousand simple, even primitive people (whom I had always instinctively feared, even before the war, rightly assuming that they might reject me, a mama's boy, because all this chatter about literature, the values of the intelligentsia, which ennobled me in the eyes of my social class, outside of my class did not justify my clumsiness)—so I felt terribly estranged. So often I would hear then: "Look at this young master! His little hands aren't used to working!" People behaved harshly, started up fights while lining up for food; sometimes they beat each other up. Life was stripped of the civility characteristic of my milieu.

I was constantly tired and disoriented. Wdowiński took care of me, was well disposed toward me, but he kept a distance, and I understood that I could not come closer to him emotionally. I tried to get used to loneliness. Loneliness, by the way, afflicted not only me but all the people in the camp. They talked about their families, showed each other pictures, cried—they missed their families. That feeling dominated; it was stronger and more difficult to bear than fear.

Meeting Fredek Lewin brought me great relief. A year younger and exceptionally nice, he was a boy I knew from my Jewish school. Finally, there was someone from my world, someone I could relate to and talk to. He talked on and on about his mother. He missed her terribly. I missed mine, too. We talked nonstop.

Fredek had a tough job. He had to dig, lug heavy loads. His group was taken far away from the camp. In the evenings he would lie down exhausted. He had sores on his toes; he complained that his leg hurt.

Wdowiński, who had known Fredek before the war (Fredek's dad, a lawyer, was a friend of his) was very worried about the boy's condition. When finally it was arranged to place Fredek in the camp hospital, it turned out that his toes had to be amputated.

Fredek stayed in the hospital for a week. He could not remain there any longer, so he returned to work with wounds that had not healed. Pus appeared and an infection. He had to be sent to the hospital again.

I thought about visiting him in the hospital, but I didn't have a pass and it didn't occur to me to somehow arrange for one. When a few days later I was told he had died, I was astonished. Astonished that I didn't feel a thing. Not only had I not gone to visit him in the hospital, though he had become my close friend in the camp, but now that he was dead, I felt totally indifferent. Why this sense of numbness? I wondered. I could see that Wdowiński was depressed; the death had affected him deeply. But I felt nothing. I was completely absorbed by my own existence, by the daily struggle to survive, to get food, the thing that mattered most in the camp.

All around me people were swelling from starvation and dying. We avoided death—Budzyń was not Majdanek or Treblinka, but the daily food ration, two watery bowls of soup with a slice of bread, was not enough to survive on. Those who couldn't get additional food had to die. So everybody in the camp was preoccupied with survival.

One could illegally buy bread, butter, or bacon obtained from local peasants and smuggled into the camp. Smuggling was rampant at that time since it was easy to sneak out of the camp. You could have letters delivered and matters arranged for money. Occasionally someone even escaped but rarely. There was no one to escape to and nowhere to go.

I remembered one smuggler from Warsaw, by the name of Neuman. He used to buy things from my grandfather. Now, thanks to him, Wdowiński regularly received money and food from his friends in Warsaw. I, too, received the first sum of money while in the camp through Neuman. He found the Pole to whom Grandfather had given some paintings for safekeeping and that Pole forwarded seven hundred zloty for me.

For seven hundred zloty, one could live a month and a half without starving. A loaf of bread cost twenty-five zloty; a kilogram of bacon about seventy zloty. People translated everything then into daily and weekly portions of food.

The labor camp for Jews in Budzyń had already existed for a year. We, the new arrivals from Warsaw, numbered about two thousand. The old inhabitants (mostly from Kraśnik and environs) were as numerous. And the old ones lived better than we did because they were familiar with the camp and knew how to climb up the ladder of camp privileges.

Only a few Germans ran the camp. All the administrative jobs were performed by Jewish functionaries (there were about two hundred of them), and they constituted the most privileged group of prisoners. They had a better barrack, a better kitchenette, and they received a lot of food. Doctors were another special group. They lived separately (Wdowiński soon moved in with them), received double portions of bread, and because they treated not only prisoners but camp administration as well, they did not lack for food.

Some of the Jewish functionaries in Budzyń were from Kraśnik; some were POWs, that is, Jews who had served in the Polish army and were taken prisoner after the September 1939 campaign. Compared to Jewish functionaries from other camps, the POWs were exceptional. They didn't humiliate us; they even protected us (it was their boss, Sztokman, who at the very beginning saved my life); they kept information about prisoners' escapes from the Germans and, overall, maintained a particular inner resistance against them.

They had their own morality and sense of justice. I remember a cruel lynching—ordered by Sztokman—of a Budzyń prisoner who had previously been a Jewish policeman and extorted huge bribes from Jews in exchange for not taking them to the Umschlagplatz. On another occasion the POWs arranged a public beating of a prisoner who had stolen something from another prisoner.

The POWs respected Wdowiński a great deal, not only as a doctor but as an important political figure with a well-known prewar record. Wdowiński collaborated closely with Żabotyński, the leader of the rightist Zionist Jewish Revisionist Party, and in 1919, during the Polish-Ukrainian fights for Lwów, as a mere twenty-year-old, he organized Jewish self-defense against Polish and Ukrainian pogroms. Later, the Polish authorities sentenced him to death for these activities, but an international furor arose, and Wdowiński was ultimately released. In the camp he was a legend. And since he took care of me as if I were his son and everybody saw that, I was assigned easier jobs.

For the first few days I worked in the kitchen, so I wouldn't be too noticeable with my leg in cast. (Had Feiks seen me again with that cast, I would not be alive. He was a psychopath. He killed for just about anything, even a louse crawling on one.) Since the daily peeling of potatoes tired and bored me, the cook let me go sometimes, and I stayed alone in the barrack. That was not safe because Feiks prowled around the camp; he rode a terribly noisy motorcycle looking for loafers like me. Yet I preferred hiding from Feiks to peeling potatoes. When Feiks was riding to one end of the camp, I dashed to the other. When he entered the barrack on the right, I rushed to the one on the left, and I had the feeling that as long as I kept track of his movements, he would not catch me.

There was no systematic extermination in Budzyń. The mere fight against starvation, however, could end in the loss of one's life. Because, from time to time, Feiks and his assistants searched prisoners, and if money or illegal food were found, one was in danger of severe beating or death. (Feiks not only killed on impulse, he also relished holding public cautionary executions.)

And yet the smuggling continued. It was the only chance one had to stay alive. Although the Ukrainians made the smuggling difficult (their only charge was to watch us so we wouldn't escape from the camp, but they enjoyed searching us for money), still one could manage it because they applied the "half and half" rule. When they found some money, they made an offer: give it up voluntarily and we'll take half and leave you half. If you don't, we'll take it all and we'll beat you up to boot.

Of course, they didn't denounce us to the Germans. That would have deprived them of the income derived from us.

Two weeks after my arrival in Budzyń, they took my cast off, and, like most people, I started going to work outside the camp, where on vast grounds stood buildings constructed by the Poles before the war. The Germans were organizing an airplane factory there. Since they called the place Heinkelwerke, they probably intended to produce Heinkel airplanes.

Most often, I dug something, pushed a wheelbarrow (Wdowiński constantly made sure I was given easier tasks); for a while I also worked outside of Heinkelwerke, in the woods. One occasionally went there without any guards, so it was very easy to escape.

One man who worked with me started talking me into a joint escape. We'll sleep in the forests, he said. As to food, we were to plead with Catholic priests, who, according to him, were supposed to be more given to compassion toward Jews than regular Poles. Yet when I mentioned this plan to Wdowiński, he merely shrugged his shoulders. "If you wish, run away. It seems hopeless to me. How will you make it without any help, without contacts with the Poles?" I responded that I wanted to hide in Warsaw. "In Warsaw? Who do you expect to help you there?!"

Wdowiński convinced me. The man escaped by himself.

When, after Fredek Lewin's death, Marceli Stark, the mathematician from Lwów, ended up sharing my bunk, an important period of camp life began for me. Stark was close to dying because he had no money whatsoever, and, to avoid starvation, he searched in the garbage for scraps of food. Eating the scraps made him nauseous, but he saw it as his only chance to survive.

I was intrigued by the fact that he was a mathematician, and I asked him some naive mathematical question. He was delighted that someone was interested in math and, using a stick, started writing equations in the sand. And then he started telling me about his life in Lwów, about Ukrainian literature, which he loved very much, and a kind of friendship developed between us—between him, the tottering intellectual close to death, and me, the high school student manqué and math lover.

In no time, we were joined by an engineer, Zysman, a very sophisticated man who knew literature, philosophy, and math and physics (he had a great influence on me). And then I also met Karol Lindner, a Trotskyist. And our discussions began: about Żeromski, about Ilya Ehrenburg, about Plato, about World War I. They summarized books for me, recited poems; Zysman explained the Newtonian system to me; Lindner expounded Trotsky's theory of permanent revolution; Stark taught me calculus. . . .

I was sixteen years old then. Stark was about thirty-five, and Zysman about forty. They seemed to enjoy educating me.

Did we have any awareness that we would die soon? Yes. But we didn't have a sense it would happen soon, tomorrow. There was a certain normalcy in all of that. Wake up at 6 A.M., roll call at 7 A.M., march to work under the supervision of the Ukrainians, soup (a liquid with pieces of half-rotten cabbage or frostbitten potatoes) at noon, then work again, our count by the Jewish "capos," return to camp, evening roll call (sometimes terribly long), finally, at 8 P.M., the second soup and a half pound slice of bread, and—at 10 P.M.—the day was over. There was little time for conversations.

And yet, what I remember best from Budzyń are these conversations, not the boredom and the tedium of the daily ten-hour-long work, not the constant thinking about food, but precisely that we are sitting somewhere and chatting about literature, about Balzac, about this and that.

Yes, we knew we were on vacation from death, but it didn't stop me from sitting down with Stark, when occasionally we were given some free time on a Sunday afternoon, to talk about mathematical logic. Even when one is sure of one's death, one doesn't think only about surviving or escaping. One has other functions, not only physical functions.

After a while I came to realize that there were some interesting people in the camp. There was Wolfson, the high school principal and Yiddishist, for instance, and his son, a few years older than me. They were handsome men, tall, with intelligent faces, purebred intellectuals. Their love was the Jewish culture of the diaspora. They claimed that Jews should cultivate it. They reminded me a little of my father, who liked Jewish folklore so much.

Wdowiński appreciated the Wolfsons, but as a Zionist he was ideologically unsympathetic to their views. He rejected the values of diaspora culture because he believed that life under the rule of other nations and countries caused the degeneration of the Jewish nation, and until Jews proudly, with weapons in their hands, conquered their own territory, they would be scorned and attacked by other nations. "Jews are an abnormal race!" Wdowiński pontificated peremptorily. "If one has the mentality of a conquered man, one cannot be mentally healthy."

The question why no one liked us, the Jews, preoccupied me still in the ghetto. I saw that our fate was different, that we were dying differently, and once I asked Wdowiński if it were true the world was happy that we were being killed. He said it was true to a certain extent. "Anti-Semitism is a natural phenomenon," he explained to me.

"People are anti-Semites not because they are bad but because no country can allow for its important economic domains to become dominated by another nationality."

Sometimes Wdowiński used me as an example of deformed Jewishness. "Truth be told, what kind of Jew are you?! You don't speak Yiddish; you don't speak Hebrew; you never read the Bible; you don't know your own nation's past."

I didn't like what Wdowiński was saying, but he made no allowances for any discussions. Actually, even in my thoughts I couldn't come up with any counterarguments to his reasoning. I wasn't anthropologically sophisticated enough then to respond to him: "Yes, my language is Polish, and yet I represent the Jewish nation." I only asked myself: "Weren't Zysman and Stark, whose language was also Polish, true Jews? Were the simple people around me who so often scolded me—'Red Yiddish! Speak Yiddish! Don't speak Polish! That's not our language!'—more genuine Jews?"

In camp conversations I often heard the annoying, nationalistic judgments that we, the Jews, were more valuable than other nations; we suffered more and deserved greater respect. Wdowiński didn't think so, but others often said so. I remember my helplessness in a discussion with a certain pharmacist who was trying to prove that Jews had more kindness and more humane impulses than Poles. I disagreed with him hopelessly, gave him counterexamples, but I could see that he liked his stereotypes because, thanks to them, he could feel better and smarter.

At such moments I was overcome by anger that I couldn't counter such nonsense with my own, equally decisive worldview. Yet, I couldn't. It troubled me. I knew less and less well where I belonged. I looked at the few thousand Jews with whom I shared my fate and—truthfully—my attitude toward them was not very friendly.

In late fall the Germans organized a several-week-long course in Budzyń to train young prisoners in metalworking. (It was some German madness: on the one hand, they were finishing us off, and on the other, teaching us a trade. The left hand didn't know what the right one was doing!) Fifty of us in the age bracket of seventeen to twenty were chosen. (Wdowiński recommended me.) All the training consisted of was learning to use dull files to smooth out some holes in iron bars. They didn't teach us about any tools, gave us no lectures. It was just tedious standing and filing for eleven hours a day. I was one of the worst students of that school.

Five masters—"Volksdeutsch" Germans from Yugoslavia—supervised us. Two of them were brutal and abused people they considered poor workers (fortunately, I was not under their supervision), but the remaining three gave the impression of normal, traditional craftsmen. If they happened to slap someone, they did it in a routine manner, the way a good craftsman rebukes his apprentices.

The chief master, *Obermeister* (also in the category of a traditional craftsman), came to be very fond of one of us, a student of a rabbinical school from Kraśnik, and after work he often took him to his room to chat (no, there was nothing sexual about it). The boy spoke Yiddish; the master spoke German; they understood each other. Once, the master asked the boy what he thought of Hitler. "Hitler is a bandit," the boy responded without hesitation. To which the master replied: "Perhaps Hitler is a bandit to a certain degree; still he is a great man." That's how they conversed.

Various interactions occurred in the camp between the prisoners and those who imprisoned them. For instance, a violinist, Flato, a wonderful virtuoso, would have starved if it weren't for the Ukrainians. He had no money whatsoever, but the Ukrainians, who liked music very much, kept inviting him to their lounge and gave him food in exchange for his playing.

An interesting event was the farewell to Feiks. (He was transferred elsewhere.) Feiks gathered us all for a roll call and said he was bidding us farewell and was thinking with pleasure about the time he had spent with us because he saw us on the right path to spiritual regeneration. Then he asked us if there were any performers among us (a few came forward), and he decided that on this last evening of his we would have a common performance.

The prisoners built a dais for Feiks upon which he sat like on a throne. Someone sang a song; someone performed a skit. Feiks applauded everything politely, and we, the whole camp (attendance was mandatory), sat on the grass in a slight stupor. Here was the fellow who treated us with such cruelty, this murderer, who was now saying that he was sorry to leave us because he had grown attached to us and was moved. I had the feeling of total absurdity.

One day, however, I found that absurdity—the absurdity of the twisted executioner-victim relationship—in myself. It was in the fall, when I was sent as a boy "factotum" to assist two electricians (one was a Pole, hired in the camp as a free man; the other was a prisoner, a Jew from Holland). Suddenly, I felt envy that the Dutch Jewish prisoner was working for the Germans as a qualified electrician while I was just a drudge. I went as far as to steal the electricity textbook from the pocket of the Polish electrician's coat. (I thought that if I reviewed the textbook, in a few hours I would know everything and I could say I, too, wanted to be an electrician). I got into trouble, of course. The electrician started looking for the book, started yelling, everybody was searched, and finally they caught me. They could have shot me for that!

Fortunately, I merely ended up being fired because Wdowiński interceded on my behalf. And the question arises: where did that paranoid ambition of mine to be a good qualified worker in a German concentration camp come from? I myself wonder.

Time passed. I came to know several interesting peers of mine. There was Emil Wertheim from Warsaw, a remarkably intelligent boy; like me, he liked physics and math. We engaged in many discussions. There was Rysiek Krakowski, also from Warsaw, a man of exceptionally friendly and serene demeanor. I met a musician from the eastern territories. He was a village musician, but he also knew classical music and sang to us. He sang Beethoven, Chopin. And I met another very exceptional boy from the eastern parts, a type that no longer exists today! He came from some small provincial place, spoke only Yiddish and Belorussian; his only education and the only thing he read was the Talmud, and yet he was very open-minded, sensitive, and intelligent.

My conversations with that boy were very interesting. For, although we came from two different worlds, we communicated very well. He based every argument of his on the Talmud, and I remember him saying once to me: "Math can be beautiful—the axioms, the unfolding of mathematical thought—but it's not as beautiful as the Talmud. Because in math you have a solution. It's proven once and for all, but in the Talmud nothing is proven once and for all. At any moment someone can demonstrate that something is different. Everything can be subjected to a new interpretation. It's a closed system but infinitely rich."

I was struck by it. "How come"—I thought—"in our Western rationalism we aim for absolute certitude, and here comes someone who claims that something is better because it cannot be proven?" It was like an anthropological difference, a difference of cultures! We represented two structurally different systems of thought, and yet, despite that, it was possible for us to exchange ideas. Something like that happened to me for the first time in my life.

In the fall of 1943, it was decided that a project bureau employing prisoner-draftsmen would be launched at the Heinkelwerke. Stark was entrusted with the management of the bureau, and Zysman became its chief designer. The original intent was to employ only draftsmen in the bureau, but Stark and Zysman persuaded the Germans that auxiliary personnel also had to be hired to do various calculations. (The point was, of course, that winter was coming and it was worth trying to place as many people as possible under a roof, in the unheated, but, nevertheless, closed building.)

In no time, the bureau was filled with people assembled by Zysman. These were largely members of the intelligentsia (they supported each other in the camp). I shared a room, among others, with a very affable high school student, Orensztajn, and his sister, a beautiful girl. The Orensztajns came from a doctors' family in Hrubieszow.

There was nothing for us to do in the bureau. We played games, invented various ways of pretending to be doing something, talked, and joked. The biggest challenge was not to freeze and not to fall asleep out of boredom.

When the Russian front began approaching, the idea arose in my mind that I would escape when the Russians were nearby. I would hide in the forest and wait for them. I looked at the German cargo trains that were departing from our factory, going east, and I thought: "I'll find out when such a train is leaving; I'll buy some bread and bacon; at the last moment I'll hide in the freight car. . . ."

Of course, as usual for me, these were merely pipe dreams. In fact, I did not want to escape without Wdowiński. And Wdowiński had been thinking about escaping for a long time. The escape motif surfaced during the entire stretch of my camp existence. Everybody knew that for now we remained alive because the Germans needed us. Sooner or later, however, they would liquidate us. And our problem was not how to survive the camp but how to escape from it.

There was a good chance for a successful escape with Wdowiński because the London government had decided to save him. Wdowiński established contacts with the government through Neuman and a Polish woman deeply devoted to Wdowiński. The agreement was that he himself would arrange his exit from the camp, and the Home Army would prepare a hiding place for him in the village. But while the plan for his escape was maturing, a new German commander took over the camp and ordered all prisoners to be divided into groups of ten with the escape of one prisoner being punished by the shooting of the entire group of ten.

The commander meant what he said. In no time the first group execution took place. Wdowiński abandoned his plan at that time. He would never decide on other people dying because of his escape.

One day it was suddenly announced that the following day we would be evacuated to another nearby camp. It was winter. The Russian front was approaching rapidly.

Nobody believed in the "nearby camp." Everyone was persuaded that it was not going to be an evacuation but death. We knew that the camp at Trawniki was liquidated, Poniatowa and Majdanek as well. Now it was our turn.

I remember very well our last night at the Budzyń camp. I was lying in my bunk and thinking: "They'll kill me tomorrow. Probably as early as tomorrow morning, but I still have the whole night of living ahead of me. Well, it's still so much—the whole night!"

The "nearby camp" turned out to be a reality. The living conditions were even better than in the previous camp. Also, one didn't see any dying people there. Those who didn't have any money had died a long time ago. And those who remained among the living either had money or had other means of survival.

The physical aspect of camp life was not very difficult for me. Something else was difficult: the fatigue born of boredom and hopelessness, the awareness that everything proceeded toward an unequivocal end. I was convinced that Grandma, Grandpa, and Jędruś were no longer alive, that there were probably no Jews left at all. "Perhaps only

Mother"—I thought—"saved herself in Warsaw." I didn't know what Wdowiński knew, that a moment after their escape from Umschlagplatz my mother and Aunt Ala ran to the right, to the Werteerfassung warehouse, and some German discovered them there and shot them.

Wdowiński obtained that information thanks to Neuman, but he kept silent. He was afraid I would collapse. And I continued to live with the thought that perhaps my mother was still alive somewhere.

At a certain moment—late in the spring of 1944, when the Russians were quite near—they started gradually transferring us to other camps. Every few days a team would come and announce the need for volunteers: "Who would like to go to the camp in Płaszów? Who'd like to go to Mielec?" (This way we were finding out that west of us there were still some camps with Jews). When there weren't enough volunteers, the administration assigned prisoners to be transferred. Sometimes they announced the need for particular professions: electricians, mechanics, people with high school diplomas. At times it seemed as if an employment agency came to us.

The volunteers were leaving, but Wdowiński and I remained stuck in place. I asked him why we didn't volunteer, and he responded repeatedly: "There's a principle. Stay in the old camp and don't choose. You can't trust the Germans. If they tell you that something will be better, it definitely won't be better."

We remained until the moment when, in June of 1944, everybody in the camp was packed into cattle trains and taken away.

The trip was not terrible. There was enough room for everyone. We were being taken to Radom, not knowing at all what to expect.

❖

IO

The camp in Radom I don't remember at all. I don't recall my camp mates nor who I shared my bunk with nor any conversations. All I remember is work. Twelve hours a day at the assembly line in the weapons factory.

Try to stand every day for twelve hours at the assembly line. Everything is arranged there so that you constantly pull something in or out, put something on or take something off. If you make a mistake, the mistake is carried further down.

People were tortured for such mistakes, beaten so badly some of them died.

I had a job in the Puch Dennler factory, which produced guns. I stood next to the assembly line horrified by my own clumsiness. I couldn't keep up. At any moment I could have been accused of sabotage (the slightest blunders were treated as such).

I was careless, terribly tired. It was becoming dangerous. Finally, a prisoner who stood next to me at the assembly line and played the role of an assistant/instructor told the foreman, after a few days, that I had to be transferred because I was delaying the work of the entire group. That's what saved me.

My new job, although not assembly-line work, was also horrible. I had to file the outer surfaces of gun barrels, holding them with bare hands and using a tool resembling a crank. The surfaces were rough and jagged so I constantly injured my hands. On a number of occasions, I asked our Polish foreman for protective gloves or at least a rag. He just growled in response. Finally, on one occasion he said in rage: "When we were toiling to have some black bread, your mother fed you challah. Now see for yourself how much fun work is!" This had the flavor of working-class vengeance of sorts. Well, at least he didn't resort to hitting.

It was said of the Radom camp that it was affluent. People weren't starving there; the food was better than at Budzyń. An extra portion of soup was always a possibility. There were no searches; one didn't see any marauding Ukrainians, so the black market, although forbidden, was flourishing.

Unfortunately, I could not take advantage of it because I ran out of money. So did Wdowiński. What's more, he no longer had any privileges. There the privileged status was based either on connections with the Radom Jews in the camp administration, and they had already formed their own semifamilial elites a long time ago (I recall the big families—the Goldbergs, the Adlers, the Frenkiels), or one had to belong to the group of Radom craftsmen. (There were entire professional clans of local printers and tanners in the camp who worked for the Germans and received better housing and better food, and when a new craftsman from Radom arrived, in no time he became a member of the clan.)

The Radom camp administration struck me as repulsive. The Jewish functionaries there were only concerned with their own interests and often, without any scruples, acted as flunkies to the Germans. I saw the remaining people in the camp as a foreign, provincial mass, and I wasn't attracted to them at all. Perhaps there were some members of intelligentsia among them, but I had no energy left to look for them. I don't even remember if I talked to Wdowiński. I was so tired after being on my feet for twelve hours that each day I just dreamed about the night coming and about collapsing on my bunk.

I had lived in camps for a year and a half by then, and my supply of energy was really getting exhausted.

One day the camp suddenly shut down. A hasty evacuation was ordered. The Germans chased everybody out onto the highway and made us march toward Tomaszów Mazowiecki. This was August 1944. The Russians were already near Warsaw.

We were several thousand people marching on the road. The heat was unbearable. We walked days on end without water, without food.

People were fainting, mostly women and the elderly. The Germans killed anyone who fell and didn't get up.

I walked next to Wdowiński, who kept repeating, "We have to be up front! It's dangerous to be in the back!" But I was limping. I had an old shoe with a protruding nail and developed a pus-filled blister on my heel.

Occasionally the column would stop by a spring or a lake. Once, we were allowed to bathe in a river. The sun was shining; the water glimmered. I wondered, should I swim down the river and escape? The dogs wouldn't pick up my scent. That's what I thought, but I felt too weak. Besides, how could I possibly hide with the big red cross on the back of my clothes and without any money?

On our way we passed groups of deserters from the Russian Army who were now incorporated into the German troops. These were entire ethnic divisions—various Kalmucks, Uzbeks, men from the Caucasus, Azerbaijan. Slant-eyed, they looked strange in the German army.

One morning, I woke up and fainted. Wdowiński tried to revive me, slapped me on the face, stood helpless. I finally got up, but I could walk only with great effort.

The blister on my foot bothered me terribly. I dragged myself. Wdowiński didn't abandon me. More and more rows of people moved ahead of us, and I kept walking more and more slowly.

Every once in a while, we heard a gun shot in the back of us. I knew these were shots aimed at those who had fallen down. About three hundred people had already been killed on the road that day. Wdowiński attempted to support me, but I was staggering.

The final rows of people were already close by. That meant death. Finally, Wdowiński made up his mind: "I'm going ahead." And he did. He had done an awful lot for me, but had he stayed now, he would have died in vain.

I remained alone. And suddenly, I had an upsurge of energy. I pulled myself together, clenched my teeth, and charged forward. I wasn't killed.

Four days later we reached Tomaszów at long last. We were crammed into an empty factory hall. I felt incredibly tired. I lay down on the floor. It was hard but felt like deliverance.

Fortunately, they didn't march us anywhere. We were given some water and most likely some bread as well. We were waiting for transportation. One day went by, another, a third, and a fourth. I was resting.

A few days later the trains arrived. We were loaded into cars. I sat next to Wdowiński. We wondered where we were going this time. At last, people by the window determined that the direction was southwest. So it was Auschwitz. I asked Wdowiński if we would be killed there. He just lowered his head and said: "Alas."

The car wasn't too crowded. I could sit; I could lie down. I knew it would be a few more hours before we reached Auschwitz, which meant I had a few more hours of living ahead of me.

There had already been so many times I was supposed to die in a matter of hours! I knew very well the peculiar sense of time at such moments. It always felt like a very long while. I had another day, another night, a few more moments to be alive. . . .

Several times already I had wondered what that death would be like. Several times already I had tried to imagine it—and I couldn't. I was afraid. Not afraid of the way they would kill us, not afraid of the pain or its vehemence, but afraid of death itself. I was afraid of the transition from life to death.

❁

I I

The train stopped at Auschwitz. From the window I saw naked women going somewhere. The Germans yelled at us "Raus! Get out!" and a selection followed. If there was a "selection," there was some hope.

I saw the elderly being left behind, those who looked weak being left behind, women, too. I passed! Somehow they didn't stop me.

They herded us onto the train. Wdowiński was there. We waited full of anxiety. At last the train moved.

I didn't know if I should rejoice yet. I couldn't believe it. And yet the train did move. We were leaving Auschwitz. And it was then that for the first time in a very long while the thought crossed my mind— "Maybe I'll survive the war." I was in the very eye of death and I was leaving! I was going away!

We were heading for Germany. And I wanted one thing only—to leave Poland, the danger zone, as soon as possible. If I got away, I'd be saved.

I don't know where this thought came from. As it turned out, it was in Germany that I was closest to losing my life.

We were let out in a camp near Stuttgart, in the town of Vaihingen an der Enz. The camp was desolate. There were no prisoners yet. Everything was new—new bunks, new barracks, and under the open sky, new wash basins made of stone. This Spartan style made a good impression on me.

A few days later I realized what a horrible camp it was and how terribly hard the construction work was that we had to do. I had to load some stuff onto freight cars, push wheelbarrows. The German foremen were capable of beatings, of cruelty.

I was terribly hungry. I thought of nothing but food. The daily ration was two hundred grams of bread and two portions of watery soup. No smuggled food was available (because one couldn't smuggle anything from the local Germans); there were no privileges. The only ones who had privileges were the cooks and a few Jews from the former Radom administration (the Radom hierarchy survived here partially).

One day Wdowiński was taken away. The question had been posed: "Are there any doctors here?" He came forward and was taken to another camp.

I stayed behind alone. The nights were cold. I had a blanket, but I froze. One had to march to work for kilometers on end, through mud, over hills. It was still autumn and it kept raining. My tattered shoes got wet instantly. Dampness permeated me. I grew skinny and weak.

We went to work in the mountains, in Wittenberg. The mountains were beautiful. I liked them very much. And the rain and fog somehow seemed to fit them. It was a strange feeling, but as I waded through mud, the rain and fog in the mountains brought me great relief.

I knew the war was ending and it was just a matter of enduring. At the sight of the mountains, I felt a foreshadowing of something good, as if the rain and the fog wished to tell me something about hope.

Devastated by hunger, people were dying like flies. They succumbed to typhus, dysentery, tuberculosis. A big grave was dug behind the camp. Every day, new corpses were tossed there.

Those who stayed alive were exhausted physically and mentally to the extreme. Everybody thought of nothing but survival. The atmosphere was tense, the interactions brutal. Whenever anything was distributed—whether soup or straw for mattresses—people would fling themselves at one another and fight. All the energy was focused on physical survival.

We were given bread in the evening, none in the morning. Everybody always told me to save the bread for the morning so I wouldn't go hungry to work. But I could never do that! I would gobble up the bread in the evening and think: "Oh, how I lack willpower!"

One day I was given permission not to go to work. I was lying in the barrack, all alone, and suddenly, I began imagining how pleasant it would be to stroll in the street without a care and in the company of my grandpa from Tłomackie Street. I recalled the movie houses, the lights, Warsaw streets, and I savored these visions.

Such daydreams occurred to me more and more often. Steeping myself in the imaginary prewar world gave me great pleasure.

I fell sick with dysentery.

One could see all over the camp emaciated "Muslims," a term used in the camps to refer to people totally emaciated and close to death. The "Muslims"—weak, stinking, sometimes weeping, with feces dripping from their pants—were the embodiment of camp degradation. They were disdained. In my heart, I, too, disdained them, although I realized how unjust that was. And now I was becoming a "Muslim." Several times already I had not made it to the outhouse. I was disgusted with myself. I knew that such diarrhea spelled the end—dehydration and death. And this combination of weakness, pain, and simultaneous self-contempt was a horrible feeling for me.

Dr. Gliniewiecki, whom I had met accidentally (I knew him from the Budzyń camp), told the doctors that I was Wdowiński's protégé and a senator's grandson. That saved me. They put me in the hospital and placed me in the room for the dying. I shared a bunk with a man in agony. He died. I spent the entire first night next to a corpse. Lice walked all over me. The filth in that barrack was horrendous.

Days went by. I didn't walk in mud; I didn't carry sacks with timber; I was using very little energy. And although the hospital didn't provide any medications, my condition stabilized. One day a miracle happened—the diarrhea stopped; I climbed down from the bunk bed and started walking around the barrack.

I beseeched one of the doctors to transfer me to the room for patients who were not so sick. Many privileged, healthy people were sent there and kept illegally. They talked, played cards. The man whose bunk I was to share (Kuba Blatman, ten years older than me, later my close friend and for a long time my trusted mentor) was also healthy. He was staying there as a protégé of his cousin, Dr. Boim.

I rested, talked to Blatman, solved various mathematical equations in my head. Once, I started thinking of what Stark and Zysman had told me about Newton's theory of gravitation. Since there is general gravitation, I reflected, there must be a force of attraction. So why doesn't the moon fall upon the earth, and the earth upon the sun? I pondered this for hours and suddenly—aha!—I understood! They had some initial velocity! I was very pleased with myself. I was beginning to feel like a human being again.

When four weeks later I left the hospital, I couldn't recognize the camp. From a Jewish camp, it had turned into an international one. The whole world had been brought here: Poles, Russians, Dutchmen, Frenchmen. There were Spaniards from the Civil War, German political prisoners. There was even a German pacifist who had been imprisoned in Hitler's camps well before the war.

I shared a bunk bed with a pleasant young Pole. He told me about his attempt to escape from the Germans after the Warsaw Uprising, how he was captured and put in a camp for Poles who had taken part in the uprising, and how while there he met Wdowiński, who was the camp doctor and the only Jew.

Apparently, Wdowiński helped people as much as he could. Once, when the *Lagerfuehrer* accused him of granting too many exemptions from work, he said something for which he could have been shot: "People get little food and work beyond the limits of their endurance, so they get sick. A doctor must exempt a sick person from work." A shadow fell over my friendship with the Pole because one day someone stole the bread I had hidden in my bed. I wondered: "Did he do it? Could it be him?" Thefts in the camp were quite common, and yet I felt disappointed.

Assorted opinions about several nationalities circulated in Vaihingen. It was said that the Russians were wild but brave; that the French were weak because they let the Germans defeat them. Sometimes I found this painful to listen to because mother instilled in me a cult of France. Here, however, almost all the Jews placed their hopes in Russia, even those who experienced the horrors of Communism in the east. "It's not the Americans nor the British, who are defeating the Germans; it's the Russians," the Jews used to say. Given their awful experience of the Fascist world, Communism held no terror for them. Of course, the French Communists imprisoned in the camp were also full of admiration for the Russians.

In my barrack I lived next to French anti-Fascists. They were exceptionally spirited. Despite the hunger and the terribly difficult camp life, they sang; they rejoiced. I admired them, though they offended me once by their decision to boycott an Italian by the name of Guido whom I had befriended. The twenty-year-old Guido had tuberculosis. (He knew he was going to die; he couldn't eat, so he would give me his soup, which I, despite my pangs of conscience and fear of contracting tuberculosis, would end up eating.). Guido was an anti-Fascist and had been an Italian partisan. The French boycotted Guido because he was an Italian. (After joining forces with Germany, Italy treacherously attacked France in 1940). It never occurred to them that because of his fight against the Fascists he was suffering just like them.

I encountered similarly fierce nationalism in another barrack, where an old doctor was dying. He was also a Frenchman, who earlier had helped people in the camp a great deal (he, too, was very kind and fatherly toward me), and now he could no longer get up. I sat by his bed, offered him some water. At one point, as I recall, Berger, a Jew from Radom, addressed me rather brutally: "Why are you helping that anti-Semite? Haven't you heard what he says about the Jews?"

Indeed, the Frenchman did say he disliked Jews and would never permit his daughter to marry one. Yet his anti-Semitism was old fashioned, without any aggression, and I knew he was a good man. So why would I choose to reject him? Should my attitude toward anyone depend on whether that person liked Jews? Should I divide the world into anti-Semites and non-anti-Semites? Should I have such a ghetto mentality?

Meeting various nationalities at the camp—the first contact with non-Jewish groups in my life—was an extremely important experience for me. It intensified my dislike of the "judeocentric" vision of reality, a dislike I had begun developing during my conversations in Budzyń. Now it was enormously important for me to have come to realize that not only Jews but also members of other nationalities could be humiliated and debased victims; that I could become good friends not only with Jews but also with people of other nationalities; that I could admire even deeply devout Christians, whom earlier—remembering the prewar ant-Semitic pamphlets by Father Trzeciak—I had always suspected of narrow anti-Semitism. The Christians whom I so admired were the Dutch Protestants. They, unlike the other prisoners at Vaihingen, didn't fling themselves at the soup, didn't fight for survival, didn't steal, but read the Bible constantly, prayed in concentration, and although they were starving and dying like everyone else, I saw in them the triumph of the spirit over the body.

The mental ghetto to which Berger and Jews like him were committed repelled me. I remember to this day the sense of disgust I felt when a well-fed, privileged Jew from Radom came to our barrack once and offered some food to Kertes, an exceptionally sophisticated Hungarian Jew. Kertes thanked the plump man politely and the latter, all puffed up, replied: "That's how we, Polish Zionists, behave."

I didn't want to identify with such Jews for anything in the world.

After bombardments, we were often taken to Stuttgart and other cities to remove the rubble. One night, we were struggling mightily to push a cart filled with debris in some small town. The town was asleep. And then some elderly German woman, who must have been woken up, leaned through the window and, seeing how we were struggling and how harshly we were being treated by the supervising SS man, yelled at him angrily: "And why aren't you pushing? Why aren't you helping them?" I saw that there were Germans averse to what was being done to us.

Blatman met very distinctive Germans when he, along with a group of thirty other Jews, went to work at the estate of the baroness von Neurath. (The von Neuraths were a well-known aristocratic family from Wittenberg.) The baroness noticed that Blatman spoke good German and began asking him about conditions in the camp. She was moved by what he told her. She took Blatman into her house (that was categorically forbidden!), offered him lunch, and promised that she would try to persuade the *Lagerfuehrer* that it was in his interest to treat us better because the war was coming to an end.

During the following days, the baroness talked to Blatman daily, gave him food, and soon her daughter, a beautiful sixteen-year-old girl, fell in love with him. One day the baroness volunteered to arrange for Blatman's escape. Blatman didn't accept the offer because had he done so, his cousin, Dr. Boim, would be shot. So he stayed in the camp.

Winter was almost over. I worked infrequently in those days. There wasn't enough work for everybody. Also, the amount of food we were given was decreasing steadily.

One could feel the end of the war approaching. One day I saw the anti-Fascist Frenchmen lean out the window and yell to the Fascist Frenchmen who were watching us from the prison towers (because in this camp it was the Fascist French that watched us): "Hey, you! The war is almost over! When it's over, we'll make cutlets out of you!" The latter yelled something in reply, but one could see they were afraid. We had the psychological advantage. The front was near; the cannons were within earshot.

The camp ended suddenly. It was on April 5, 1945. Unexpectedly, the Germans started yelling: "Everybody out of the barracks! Line up in rows! Evacuation!" The moment had come for me to undertake a life or death decision—do I leave the barrack or do I stay under the bed?

I decided not to leave, although the Germans could have entered any moment and would have killed me. Earlier, they would have certainly done so, but I figured that at the end of the war they would not opt for a massacre. An additional reason to stay was Guido, bedridden with TB. I stayed.

I sat on my bunk bed and listened up. Outside, there was commotion, shouting, until, after a few hours, the march started and everything quieted down. There was a silence. Nothing interrupted it.

I kept listening. All night and all morning, there were no noises. Suddenly, a dentist from Radom whom I knew, entered the barrack. He said there was a big pile of potatoes behind the camp and we should go and get some for the others. It turned out that quite a few people had hidden in other barracks, but, like me, they sat quietly and didn't stick their noses outside.

I followed the dentist. About ten of us were walking. The camp was empty, not a living soul around, no Germans. Supposedly a German SS doctor wearing the Red Cross armband was spotted.

We were walking cautiously, looking around all the time. We approached the gate. No one was guarding it. We opened the gate. No guards. The watchtowers were empty. . . .

Two days later the French Army entered. It was a strange army. The soldiers were blacks and Arabs from the French colonies. Only the officers were French. They walked around the camp, saw us—the skeletons, saw the drifting and staggering "Muslims." They met their terribly emaciated French compatriots. They were shown the mass grave in which there were also many of their countrymen. They were astounded, horrified. They grew so angry they were beside themselves.

All of a sudden the German doctor with the Red Cross armband turned up and saluted the Frenchmen as if he were giving them a briefing. Astonished, the Frenchmen waved their hands, shouted, pushed him. In the end they summoned someone. A moment later I saw two black soldiers lead the doctor aside. I heard the gunshot.

That was the end of the camp at Vaihingen.

The Frenchmen dragged the entire population of the town into the camp. They continued to be furious. They pointed out to the Germans the dying prisoners, the still open mass grave with corpses arranged layer on top of layer. At last, they asked the townspeople to select a group of men for the cleanup of the camp.

The Germans started working, and it was then that the mayhem began. Now it was the prisoners who wanted to torment the Germans. I remember that distinctly. Among the men cleaning the camp was an elderly gentleman, a bit hunched, who seemed like a decent man with an intelligent face (someone said he was a teacher). The prisoners pushed him around, spat at him, prodded him. He staggered.

I felt uneasy. I pitied that man. I wanted the prisoners to stop pulling him about. What was more, among those who pushed him was a "capo" from the camp, one who used to beat us, the prisoners. I thought to myself then: "What's going on? It's on him that we should be taking revenge!" However, when the German nicknamed Yellow Jacket (*Gelbe Jacke*), who had supervised work in our camp and was known for cruelty, was being killed, I, too, felt like joining in. I felt a terrible rage. People surrounded the German from all sides and whacked him with sticks for about twenty minutes. Finally, he fell down motionless, but they continued to kick him. Then he died.

I badly wanted to see the scoundrel dead.

The next day the rumor spread that the Frenchmen gave us permission to go to town and loot. "Take revenge on those Germans!" A hoard of prisoners poured out of the camp.

All of us took off. Blatman was the only one who said he wouldn't do it. While he went to save the baroness von Neurath, who had been put in prison, I followed the others. We swarmed like locusts from house to house. Petrified, the inhabitants gave us anything we asked for at once. These were women, old men, a few middle-aged persons. I dropped by a house and asked bluntly: "What do you have?" I looked into pots, into cupboards. I took noodles, bread, beans.

I felt strange in that role, uncertain. I thought: "I don't have any food; I want to have food; I can because they wronged me." Yet at the same time I felt embarrassed that these people were afraid of me. A part of me understood that it was indecent. Others looted clothing, jewelry, money. I only took food, but even taking just that, I had a sense that I was doing something inappropriate.

At the end of the day we returned to camp. The town was completely looted. I didn't hear of any rapes or murders, but the town was completely looted.

A few days after the liberation, the French declared the camp closed. "Everybody is leaving," they said. "People from Western Europe will go home. People from Eastern Europe must remain six more weeks in Germany to undergo a quarantine. You'll live in the nearby village." They were afraid we were infected with typhus and that we, the prisoners from Eastern Europe, would spread that typhus all over Western Europe.

The time came to say good-bye. The trucks pulled up. I was happy, and at the same time I was sad because Guido had just died. Besides, I had an odd incident with one of the Frenchmen imprisoned here as an anti-Fascist partisan. I had met him at work, in the camp, and we used to enjoy talking. Now, however, when I approached him to say good-bye, he unexpectedly turned stiff, said au revoir coldly, and wouldn't even shake my hand. I was surprised. It occurred to me that he might have been an anti-Semite. He interacted with me in the camp because there the situation was dangerous. Now that it was all over, he didn't want anything to do with me, a Jew.

We climbed into the trucks—Jews, Poles, Russians. We reached the village chosen for our quarantine. It was totally deserted because the French had evicted all the Germans. They were not allowed to take any of their possessions. None. We were occupying their homes. Their cows, pigs, chickens were all ours.

People deftly selected the best farms. I, slow as usual, found some shabby hut in the end and moved into it with Warchiwker, a Jew I had befriended in the camp.

There was nothing to eat in the hut. I snuck up to the house next door, where other prisoners had already moved in, and I caught a chicken. (I didn't know if I was stealing it from the Germans or from my fellow prisoners.) Warchiwker and I killed the chicken and ate it with pleasure. It was an April evening. The soil gave off a nice fragrance, and we went for a walk. The village was beautiful.

✿

12

After the liberation, more days went by. I was in a state of absolute euphoria. For so long my life had been a tedious effort to survive; for so long I had lived with the thought that I might have a few more days, another month perhaps, but then I would die. And now . . . I might even live fifty more years! Or sixty!

It was uncanny. As if the world were summoning me.

Those several weeks of quarantine were an idyllic time. There was Blatman. There was Józio Frenkiel, the intelligent and witty young fellow I had met at the hospital in Vaihingen. There was Warchiwker from Radom, who was a stooped, religious man, perhaps twenty years older than me, and amusing with that Jewish accent of his and his hooked nose. He espoused idealistic theories that people were basically good but conditions of life corrupted them, or that prostitution was improper. These ideas of his, expressed already at Vaihingen, that horrible place where the very worst in people tended to come out, sounded so anachronistic there that Blatman and I laughed at Warchiwker heartily. We would slap his back and say, "Sure, sure, you're right." We liked him very much.

Now was a time to rest. We befriended various people. We went for long walks, climbed the hills (there were such picturesque hills there); we played chess and talked.

We came to know soldiers in the French army. One of them, an Algerian, told us about his life in Africa. Another French soldier, a captain responsible for our camp, allegedly told Frenkiel (in all seriousness) that it might be necessary to organize an intercamp brothel, because after all the horrific experiences, what men needed most was women.

We laughed. It was totally idyllic. I remember my great surprise

105

when in May, all of a sudden, the French started shooting and said they were saluting the end of the war. The end of the war? The thought that the war was still going on had never crossed my mind over the past few weeks!

People started making plans. They deliberated: should they go to America, stay in Germany, travel to Palestine. Practically no one thought of returning to Poland. A lot of people said: "Poland is not our country. The Poles were pleased with what was done to us." If anyone did decide to go to Poland, it was to dig up things hidden in the ground and smuggle them to the West or to locate relatives and take them away from the place of smoldering ruins.

Everybody wondered about locating relatives in Poland, where to ask. It was a kind of hope against all odds. Basically, it was hard to expect that it would be possible to find anyone in Poland. Yet Warchiwker, who had a wife there, talked about her constantly. Blatman thought of his younger sister in Poland; I, about my mother, hoping I might find her and perhaps someone else as well.

My plans had not crystallized, but I knew I did not want to return to Poland. "There were no Jews left there," I thought. I remembered prewar Polish anti-Semitism, and, like everybody in the village, I had a sense that I would certainly be a stranger in Poland.

Reality provided us with more and more new arguments against returning to Poland. I remember that among the many patients in the village hospital, where we helped out as volunteers, there was an unconscious Polish man sick with typhus. Warchiwker took care of him. He wiped the face of the unconscious man, offered him water; sometimes he spent the whole night next to him, like a good Samaritan. A few days later the Pole regained consciousness. He didn't quite understand yet where he was. Probably he thought he was in occupied Poland, among Germans, and the nurses were German women. Then he looked up, and bent over him was Warchiwker with his Jewish face. And then the Pole, still a bit unaware, gets up and starts yelling: "He's a Jew! A Jew!" and he summoned the nurse, pointing at Warchiwker—"He's a Jew! Jude! Jude!" He wanted to denounce Warchiwker to the Germans.

Gradually, the number of people in the village decreased. A Soviet delegation came to take away the Russians who wanted to return to their homeland; a Polish delegation came to take the Poles. The Jews, however, were told in the middle of May that America had taken over custody of them from the French, and those still needing assistance could be transferred to the American zone.

A meeting with the natives of the village was arranged before we left. They were supposed to return to their homes and pleaded with us not to wreck the remainder of their possessions prior to our departure from the village. "We know what you went through," they said. "We understand your bitterness, but we beg you—don't destroy our village."

But the meeting accomplished nothing. People destroyed everything. They hacked up sofas, defecated in the middle of rooms, did everything to defile the place as much as possible. . . .

We were transferred to the American zone and settled in Langenzelle near Heidelberg, where the Americans organized a camp for displaced persons (DPs). We were quartered in a castle on a hill (it had about forty or fifty rooms); we were given food, and we didn't have to do a thing.

Those staying in the castle were almost exclusively Jews. They talked constantly about the prewar Jewish life, about Jewish towns. They sang Jewish songs and kept longing. I liked listening to these stories and songs, but I wasn't all that emotional about them. Was it because my family was more assimilated and belonged to the intelligentsia? Once, I remember, a group of Jewish female performers came to Langenzelle, and everybody was terribly excited. "Jewish girls! Yiddishe meidl!" This is what was in the air: these Jewish women are the seeds of our nation, and now is the time to take a Jewish girl and build a new life. This kind of thinking was very distant for me. "All right," I thought, "these Jewish girls are alive. That's good. It's good that anyone has survived. But why make such a mystique of it?" I didn't feel I was a member of this ecstatic collective.

I recall one conversation with Blatman at that time, which disturbed me very much. He was seeing the young von Neurath girl, who was terribly in love with him. Her mother and the whole family approved of the relationship, but he said he would marry only a Jewish girl. On hearing that, I was speechless. Such a beautiful girl! To me this was totally absurd.

At Langenzelle, the Americans entered us into the central register of displaced persons, and now people began to search for each other in earnest. They checked lists and traveled to various DP camps. Hilel

Zajdman (my grandfather's protégé, who at one point, in the ghetto, tried to arrange for citizenship in a Latin American country for my family) came to see me and said that as my famous grandfather the senator's grandson I could get a scholarship from the Agudah Party and study wherever I wanted, in Paris or London, on the condition, however, that I represent that party. I refused, of course. (I wouldn't have been able to represent the religious Agudah Party.) On my part, I went to see Wdowiński. I had been told he was in some DP camp in Bavaria.

Wdowiński was very happy to see me. I stayed with him for two days. He told me he was thinking of going to Palestine, via Italy, and suggested I go with him. I replied that I had to find my mother first. It was only then that Wdowiński told me the truth about her fate. Now he could tell me. I didn't have to struggle to survive. The war was over, and I was already eighteen years old.

On the second day of my visit to Wdowiński's camp, a German string quartet was supposed to perform. As a gesture of good will, Germans from a nearby town sent their musicians to play Mozart for us. I was very much looking forward to the concert, but when the musicians arrived, Jews from that camp would not let them play at all. They shouted, threw stones, and yelled: "Throw them out!" It was so brutal and crude that I felt terribly put out and disoriented. On the one hand, I wanted to listen to the music and the fierceness of the Jews' reaction disgusted me; on the other hand, however, I shared their hatred of the Germans in a sense. And I asked myself—perhaps not altogether consciously—the following question: "Should I be hostile toward all Germans?"

Fresh in my memory was a conversation I had with a German I had met on the train when going to visit Wdowiński. He was a prisoner of war coming home from an American POW camp and he said to me: "You don't understand our nation yet. The Germans are more than Nazism. Not all Germans are Fascists." On my way back from Wdowiński's camp, I also had an encounter with a German. I was travelling at night in an empty and open freight car. The wind was blowing terribly. There were only the two of us—the tall German in the uniform of Luftwaffe and I. At one point the German approached me and asked me some questions:

"Where are you from? "I am a Polish Jew." "What do you intend to do?" "Study at a university most likely." "What will you study?" "Maybe physics." "It's cold." "Do you want my coat?" "No."

I said "no" harshly because I felt hatred toward that German and his Luftwaffe uniform. The conversation stopped. We traveled in silence. Finally, feeling tired, I lay down on the floor of the car and curled up. I was terribly cold. The German stood some distance from me and gazed into the night. At one point he turned toward me, took his coat off, and tossed it over me. I retained that in my memory. I don't know what he was thinking, but I remember that.

❁

13

My last DP camp was in Stuttgart. That's where I spent the happiest period of my life. The war was behind me, and everything was ahead of me. I went to the theater for the first time; to the opera for the first time. I fell in love. Everything was for the first time.

All around me there was agitation. People were getting ready to make money, to start businesses. And I—a bit of a bungler as usual and a sybarite—sat and read a lot, studied math, physics, and was meeting people.

It seemed to me that I could do anything. I was young. I had survived the war and regained my health. Everything was before me.

In Stuttgart, we lived in a working-class neighborhood near the railway station, in regular apartments, several people in each. There were about a thousand of us, and we occupied about twenty or thirty apartment buildings from which the Germans had earlier been evicted.

Our food was meager, so everybody tried to peddle something on the side. I didn't. I didn't feel like it. However, an acquaintance got me a job operating a copy machine at the U.S. Army administration, so I was entitled to eat in the army canteen and there the food was good.

I was eighteen years old and I sensed that with all my being. Perhaps I'd go to England or France? Maybe I would study physics and become a fervent scientist who hardly ever leaves his lab and makes great discoveries? Or would I go to Palestine? I might become a Zionist, a proud new Jew, living in his own country on his own soil and working hard as a farmer on a kibbutz. I might become a romantic intellectual living close to nature, a kind of spiritual peasant. Perhaps yet another romantic option would be available to me?

Most important to me was that my adult life have flair, that mine not be a common, middle-class existence. I often talked about that with a poet I knew, a fellow Jew from Poland. Singular and somewhat conceited, this fair-haired and dreamy-eyed lad fell in love with some German woman. He used to say that his love was symbolic of his liberation from the burden of Jewish nationalism, from the "tribe mentality." He, the Jew, loved a German and it was like Romeo and Juliet, a Montague and a Capulet. I actually liked that idea.

My visions of the future were not concrete plans but roles that I donned in my imagination like a little boy. Basically, the future wasn't important to me. It was the present that was important, deriving pleasure from everyday life in which there was no longer any danger. I went to the theater; I went to concerts; I met people, made new friends, and visited old ones, like Blatman or Frenkiel.

I was told that Zysman was hospitalized somewhere in the south of Germany (I no longer recall where) and was being treated for tuberculosis. I went to visit Zysman. He told me an incredible story that happened to Stark and him. After they left Budzyń, they were taken to the Planck Institute to work on the V2, the rockets dropped on London. The two of them were placed in a private apartment in Berlin, well fed, and escorted by guards to their office. They were all alone in the office, watched by a guard positioned outside their door. No one was allowed to contact them (German scientists were also forbidden any contacts). The guard would hand them various calculus problems on a piece of paper, and they, likewise, returned their solutions to the guard on pieces of paper.

One could hear all kinds of old stories in Stuttgart, but the most important thing continued to be what was happening then and there. I had a girlfriend, Ewa. She was from Łódź, and I had met her when I was still in Langenzelle. Now her brother-in-law suggested I go with them to Africa to smuggle morphine. Although, given my clumsiness, that was not very sensible, I agreed. I thought it would be such a manly adventure and I wanted to impress Ewa. Nothing came of smuggling morphine because we didn't make it across the border. We came back and again it was Ewa, concerts, books, theater. I liked that life of mine very much.

In the theater and during concerts, I observed the German public with great interest. It was sophisticated and intelligent. Quite often I found the German women attractive. I worked with one of them. She told me not to condemn all the Germans for what the Fascists had done; that German culture was not limited to Fascism; that the Germans were a diverse nation, and their culture consisted of many deeply humanistic trends. She talked in a subtle manner, was dignified and commanded respect. And it was the way she talked to me that made me believe her.

I started reading German newspapers and books. I met Germans who spoke with horror about Hitler, about Fascism and the extermination of Jews. I met other Germans who told me they felt guilty about World War II. I often heard them discuss this among themselves.

More and more often I was beginning to think that Fascism and anti-Semitism were aberrations in German culture, crooked roots that grew in a totally incomprehensible way. I did not think the same of Polish anti-Semitism. Among the Poles I met in Germany, I saw the same kind of anti-Semitism now that I had seen during the war and before the war. I remember traveling with a friend from Stuttgart to Karlsruhe. On the way we stopped in a Polish office to pick up food stamps. (Special offices to distribute food stamps to the Jews didn't exist yet.) One of the Poles standing in that office recognized us as Jews and addressed me in a theatrical manner, exaggerating the Jewish accent. "Mameshi," he said (which means "mommy" in Yiddish). "Excuse me?" I asked, not understanding the situation and rather surprised. And he responded with irony: "Oh, so you are not a Jew! I'm sorry, I'm very sorry!"

On another occasion we were going to Augsburg in a truck. I heard people speaking Polish. I realized they were coming from Poland, so I asked one of them: "What's going on in Poland?" He took a good look at me, saw I was Jewish, and said: "Everything's fine. Things are going well. They are beating up Jews."

I have to make one point: in those days in Germany I felt less animosity toward the Germans than toward the Poles. Most of my encounters with the Poles at that time were unpleasant. In our travels to Karlsruhe we often stopped in camps for Poles. They drank; they were loud and vulgar. Still stuck in my memory is an erotic scene between a big, unkempt man and a drunk woman—he was embracing her and she was howling wildly.

I also felt uneasy while talking to Poles. I was irritated by their tone of self-satisfaction. They bragged about this and that ("We fought at Monte Casino!"), but none of them told me, as the Germans had, "Well, we may not have behaved quite properly toward the Jews. We denounced them to the Germans; we helped them too little." The Poles had no self-criticism. They spoke about Jews exclusively with dislike.

My attitude at that time was anti-Polish, and that was understandable. A man sees only what he sees. What I saw in the Polish camps was drunken rabble and anti-Semites. I knew there were other Poles as well, like my barber Stefan or those who tried to arrange for Wdowiński's escape or my mother's acquaintance who sent me money to the Budzyń camp. But they were far away. In effect, they existed outside of my experience. My feelings and emotions were shaped by the Poles I was used to seeing.

I had my moments of melancholy. They came when I recalled my mother; when I thought of my family, which surely perished somewhere in some terrible way; when I thought of my grandmother whom I had offended so horribly in the ghetto. Those moments weren't frequent (I was very absorbed by the day to day life in Stuttgart), but when those images from the past life in the camps did surface, I felt very dejected. I would recall people ferreting in the garbage for some remnants of food, the "Muslims," who left behind them a trail of disgustingly fetid feces. I recalled myself in those days, me constantly thinking of food, me lying on the bunk bed with a corpse, me killing lice on my head, me eating soup out of the tubercular Guido's bowl. . . .

I felt disgust. I felt humiliated. I hadn't felt the humiliation in the same way while in the camps. Then, I just lived; I struggled to survive. That's all. But now, in Stuttgart, having survived and living in a civilized world, the sense of humiliation kept returning. It made itself felt and interfered with my breathing.

I was humiliated. All of us Jews had been debased in the camps. The Germans beat us, we let them beat us and we consisted of one wish only—to stay alive.

There was some talk about it among the Jews in Stuttgart. That we went like sheep to slaughter; that we have the mentality of victims; that we are like nettles—strong weeds capable of spreading and surviving even under the most difficult conditions. This comparison to nettles, full of self-contempt, was reminiscent of the Nazi propaganda posters presenting us, the Jews, as insects multiplying at a terrifying pace. I don't know if my disgust was affected by the Nazi propaganda or not. The fact is I felt disgusted. I thought we were a sorry breed of humans. All we possessed was the drive to survive; in mud, in feces, in our own debasement—just to survive.

Once, I recall, a Jewish officer, a representative of a Jewish military unit from Palestine (the unit belonged to the British Army because Palestine was still under the British mandate), came to Stuttgart. He was a Jew I was willing to accept. Tall, slim, sun-tanned, the boy wore his uniform with pride and had a kind of purity about him. He was someone totally different from the humiliated, crushed-to-the-ground mass of Jews from the camps. He was someone totally different from me.

Well, perhaps the Nazis had won a victory over me, after all. I had survived the war; I had survived the camps; I now attended concerts, absorbed culture, and I lived in a civilized world. Yet all along somewhere under my skin, I harbored the conviction of the inferiority of diaspora Jews in relation to other nations.

In relation to the Germans as well. It was not totally accidental that I liked German women more often than Jewish ones. It was not totally accidental that at one point I started thinking with horror that diaspora Jews do not belong to European civilization, that they were not Europeans because they were not a nation.

The memory of Jewish humiliation troubled me. It was a very wispy emotion, a subconscious one, a feeling that we were foul and repulsive, that we deserved to be trodden into the ground. . . .

In May 1946, I received a letter from Uncle Maurice from America. He was my father's brother and Aunt Manya's and Aunt Dora's brother. He was living in the United States now and wanted to bring me over. My uncle's letter was warm, from the heart. And now a mix of options emerged. On the one hand, my romanticism and various conceptions of an unusual life, on the other, America, where my relative, my father's brother, lived; where everything could be so simple, so effortless . . .

❀

14

Conclusion

I arrive. My uncle and his wife sit me down and ask me to recount.
For the first week I recount nonstop. My uncle keeps asking; he
can't have enough. His wife, my aunt, likewise.

I didn't hide any facts. Basically, I had nothing to hide. Still, I
couldn't bring myself to tell them I felt degraded. I knew that by not
talking about it I was falsifying my account because they were full of
admiration. In their eyes I was like a hero who went through hell and
survived. Yet my survival was totally accidental! I did nothing to survive, nothing at all! I was passive; I waited for something to happen.
I stayed close to the ground. It was as if someone simply didn't notice me.

A week later my uncle began introducing me to various American
Jews. They kept asking: "How do you like America? It's a great country, isn't it? Here you can forget about the past, about Poland. You'll
start a new life here!" This irritated me terribly. Contained in their
advice was an air of patronizing and the American sense of self-
satisfaction. Perhaps forgetting isn't such a bad idea. But how could I?
I was who I was, and my past had shaped me.

They expected from me accounts of a certain kind. What horrible
things the Germans had done, how mean the Poles were toward the
Jews, how beautiful Jewish culture was, and what a shame that all that
was destroyed by the vile Germans and horrible Poles.

I didn't want to adopt that tone; I rebelled against it inwardly. Earlier, it would not have occurred to me to defend the Poles, but now
when I saw that the American Jews wanted me to join in creating a
stereotype, to prove American-Jewish superiority on cue, I refused to

do it. So I said: "There are all kinds of Poles. Some are like this, others like that. It's difficult to generalize." They were very disappointed. That wasn't the only reason I disappointed them. My reluctance to serve up my experiences in a heroic sauce was another. "Tell us how you suffered, how the Jews suffered!" For me, however, it was not the suffering that was most horrible but the degradation. Was I now to transform it into heroism?

Soon, I stopped talking about it altogether.

To remain silent about the Holocaust was easy in America. Americans respected it: "It's unspeakable. It's such a crime. It must be hard for you to talk about it." They didn't guess the real reasons behind my silence. Besides, I was not the only one to keep silent. After the war the Holocaust was taboo in America. Although diaries started appearing and documents were collected, there were no historiographic analyses yet nor the later journalistic uproar.

In the meantime, I was attempting to get on with my life. It didn't go too well. I didn't have a good job. I would find some mindless job at a furniture factory or a lamp factory. I had no friends. My American peers—brave, energetic, fashionably dressed—made me envious. I didn't know how to establish contact with them. American Jews repelled me. I wasn't attracted to the Jewish arrivals from Europe either.

I went to the huge New York Public Library, I studied logic or philosophy books; I picked out Polish publications in the Slavic Division. Occasionally I would meet my old acquaintances from Europe. Ewa, my former girlfriend, arrived in New York. She was a married woman now. She had married a fellow whose first name was Mietek. We went to the beach together; we became a threesome of friends. What had happened to my romantic love for her was actually quite a surprise. I felt nothing. Sometimes I played chess with Mietek.

I went to the movies. I read. Whatever was published about the Holocaust—I read.

I read memoirs from the Soviet camps. Sometimes I myself wondered why I still kept reading all that. Perhaps I wanted to find out if my degradation was necessary. Was the degradation of other Jews in ghettos and camps necessary?

What distressed me all the time was the presumption that as a Jew

I was totally different and didn't belong to Europe. "The Poles belong to Europe in a Polish way," I told myself; "the Frenchmen the French way, but the Jews don't belong because they aren't a nation. So if I am not a European, who am I then?" I tormented myself. And I didn't want to be a Jew anymore. I didn't know who I might have wanted to be but not a Jew.

I don't remember when I shook off these Jewish complexes, if it was around that time or a bit later. I simply rubbed my eyes, as if I had awakened from some bad dream. "Look at this world!" I thought to myself. "Just because you're a Jew, you can't be a member of European culture?! That's some idiotic fancy!"

A man has a nightmare and, while it lasts, he's not aware it's a nightmare. Then suddenly, he wakes up. And the nightmare is over.

For a year and a half, I divided my time among the factory, the movies, and the library. Finally, I made up my mind. I filled out the application forms and enrolled at City College in New York. Physics and math were beginning to draw me in. All around me were people my age, maybe somewhat younger. I didn't have too much contact with them, but I appreciated their presence.

Time went by. I thought less and less about what Jews were like and more and more about who I was. American Protestant ethics were slowly permeating me. I stopped thinking: I am like that because Jews are like that. Not at all! You are who you are. Because it's your choice.

By accident, I happened upon a group of young Trotskyites at the college. They were different from average Americans, and I was attracted to them. I don't really know myself why I stayed with them. Was it because I felt alienated in America?

I abandoned the Trotskyites after nine years. I saw a huge dose of self-aggrandizement in their activities, and at one point it began to revolt me. Today I can no longer say if I ever sincerely believed in Trotskyite ideas or if I was simply attracted to the role of a "revolutionary." In any case, I started a completely different life style afterward.

I got married—to an American. I worked as a computer programmer. My social circle was partially American and partially—as is typical in America—multinational. I learned to search out people who were to my liking. In America, once you come to know it, it's not so difficult. In answer to "Where are you from?" I responded I was from Poland. "Are you Polish?" they persisted. "No, I'm Jewish," I replied. Usually, people were satisfied with this formula, and I myself felt no need to expand upon it.

Somehow, my Jewish problems subsided, although the memory of camp degradation remained lodged in me in some way.

At that time, in the late 1950s, the commonly held view about the passivity of Jews during the war was increasingly cast into doubt. Books were published that revealed more facts documenting Jewish resistance—Jewish uprisings and partisan actions. I familiarized myself with all that with great interest.

Somewhat later a triumphal note appeared in the Jewish circles— "We've survived to bear witness." This started annoying me terribly. I remembered too well the price of my "survival." "Survival?" I thought. What's the good of survival with such degradation? I assumed that all the hoopla about bearing witness was dictated by the wish to forget about that degradation, by the desire to squelch it, to cover it up, to replace it with a different psychological figure.

In the meantime, my life unfolded normally. Divorce, some women, many friends, occasionally hash. I had money and I enjoyed having fun. These were the late 1960s. Protests against the Vietnam War.

In the 1970s, several important things about the Holocaust came out (for instance, Lanzmann's *Shoah*), but at the same time the market was flooded with commercial TV series and books on the subject. I observed that with disgust. At that time in America, the Holocaust was turned into a business, a huge industry overindulging in symbols. The propaganda overtones of this huge production were generally the same: "The Holocaust resulted in many victims, but we have survived and we have built Israel. If it weren't for the Holocaust, we wouldn't have had the creative energy. That is why Israel spells the triumph of the Jews over the Holocaust."

Next to this political mythology, the motif of militant victimhood began to emerge in the Holocaust commerce: "We were wronged, so we are entitled to something and somebody is to blame. I have a grudge." This was repulsive to me. I remember in 1991, after the armed attack of the Russians on the Lithuanian parliament, a Lithuanian in Cambridge was collecting signatures under a petition protesting the attack. Suddenly, some Jew showed up and started yelling at that Lithuanian: "You people have murdered my grandfather! You, Lithuanians! You are murderers!" Perhaps that man's grandfather was indeed murdered by Lithuanian nationalists, but why should that keep me from supporting the Lithuanians now? That happened in the past! For the most part, the people who murdered us are dead! But I am alive, and I no longer wish to think about them, nor do I want to harbor a grudge.

I have heard that in America there are organizations of Jewish Holocaust survivors. There are some discussion and therapy groups, but I have never been attracted to them. I don't know exactly what the meetings held by those people entail, but I do hope they are not dedicated to remembering the wrongs. I have nothing against people remembering the past, and I myself do not wish to forget the Holocaust. When I see the huge machine of Holocaust commercialism, however, I think to myself: "One has to draw the line somewhere, to say stop. Let not the remembering of wrongs last till the tenth generation."

As for me, for more than ten years now I have not sought out films and books about the Holocaust. When some become very well known—like *Schindler's List* or Spiegelman's *Maus*—I see them or read them, but I try to live in the present. My settling of moral accounts with the past is over, I believe. After all, the only moral reality—that's what I feel today—is how you behave now, how you live now. All the mythologizing of the past, as has happened in the case of the Holocaust, cuts us off from the "here and now." It spawns microbes in your soul, or inflammation.

To put to an end means to forgive, despite the fact that forgiveness is often associated with tepid feelings. But one has to do something to stop the hurt and to live in an open way.

Twenty years ago I returned to Poland for the first time. A mathematician I knew, an American of Polish extraction, asked me to help him find traces of his family in Sanok. I thought to myself: "That's a good opportunity for an adventure." I went to Poland. I visited here and there.

The war ended my life in Poland. I was violently uprooted. I remember prewar Poland as a country of colossal anti-Semitism. Now I tried to have no biases. I was meeting people, Poles, Jews, mostly the intelligentsia close to Polish intellectual elites. I felt good; I was warmly received. Perhaps people in Poland are still anti-Semitic, I don't know. Yet I think that it's a sufficiently heterogeneous country to find people who will accept you.

There is only one problem—the trap of ethnic identity, of an endemic sense of belonging. It's a problem from which I managed to free myself during all those years in America. When I met Jews in Poland after the war (by the way, I was in Poland again in 1992), they either avoided talking about their Jewishness or emphasized it. Both behaviors seemed unnatural to me. And I think that in Poland I couldn't be "simply a Jew" or a "neutral Jew," the kind I am in America, the America of respect for individually chosen identities, of acceptance that "you are who you are." In Poland I would not be a Jew free from a problem with his Jewishness. And when the problem of the Jews' sense of belonging confronts me in Poland, I notice with great relief that I no longer suffer from that disease.

At the beginning of my life I had nothing but Jewishness and the Holocaust. Life, however, is a kind of whole. It brought other questions and problems along, which I've resolved, poorly or well, but they were different problems.

And yet I still have dreams. My dreams recur. One of them is about Warsaw. I return to Warsaw after the war. Perhaps it isn't even the war but some terrible event. I am close to dying. And I can't recognize the city.

Or I am awaiting my father's death. I know he has to die, but he isn't dying. Sometimes it's not my father but an uncle or another relative. I think to myself: "He is about to die; he is incurably ill"—but the man goes on living.

Yet another dream: I am sentenced to death. The verdict is in, but I am not dying, and there are constant stays of execution. . . .

Another dream: I am about to embark on a distant trip by boat. To reach that boat I have to walk somewhere, a very long distance. I wade through some wasteland; I am very tired. These are such repetitious dreams, tedious, exhausting, unpleasant, gray. . . .

But I wake up from them.

I wake up normally.

Maps

Poland and Germany at the start of 1939

- Alex's sojourns during WW II
- ▲ Concentration camps during WW II

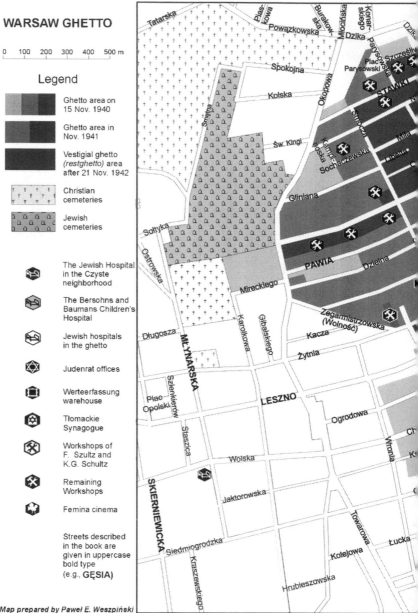

WARSAW GHETTO

0 100 200 300 400 500 m

Legend

Ghetto area on
15 Nov. 1940

Ghetto area in
Nov. 1941

Vestigial ghetto
(restghetto) area
after 21 Nov. 1942

Christian
cemeteries

Jewish
cemeteries

The Jewish Hospital
in the Czyste
neighborhood

The Bersohns and
Baumans Children's
Hospital

Jewish hospitals
in the ghetto

Judenrat offices

Werteerfassung
warehouse

Tłomackie
Synagogue

Workshops of
F. Szultz and
K.G. Schultz

Remaining
Workshops

Femina cinema

Streets described
in the book are
given in uppercase
bold type
(e.g., GĘSIA)

Map prepared by Paweł E. Weszpiński

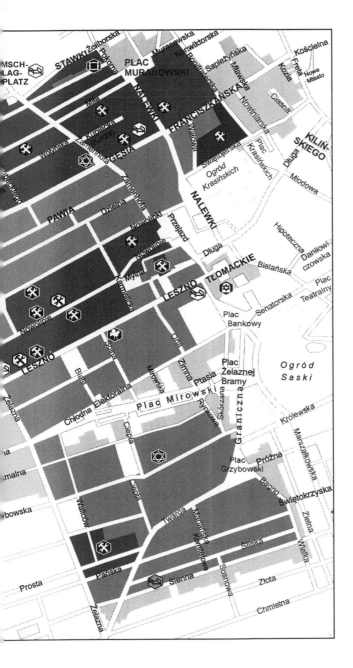

※

Author's Acknowledgments

My gratitude is owed, first and foremost, to Alex for having shared his unique story with me, thereby enabling me to embark on the fascinating adventure that the writing of this book has afforded.

I am most indebted to the translator, Professor Regina Grol, for without her energy and determination this book would never have appeared in the United States. It was she who interested the publisher in the book and made every effort to bring this project to its swift conclusion. Professor Grol has translated my book beautifully, combining literary sensitivity with an uncanny linguistic ingenuity and successfully grappling with its historical and literary substance.

I also wish to thank most cordially others who significantly aided me in my efforts to have the book published in the United States: Abraham Brumberg, Anna Frajlich, Alina Magnuska, and Marian Marzyński.

Others who in various ways assisted in the preparatory phases of the American edition and to whom I am very grateful are: Alex Bergier, Lena Bergman, Barbara Engelking, Anka Grupińska, Elżbieta Grygiel, Marek Gumkowski, Jan Jagielski, Stan Matwin, Robert Kirkland, Ruta Sakowska, Lila and Stefan Sawicki, Robert Strybel, Paweł Szapiro, and Piotr Weiser.

I am deeply indebted to Wanda Siedlecka, who provided the direct inspiration for this work by introducing me to Alex, and others who served as intermediaries in my transatlantic contacts with him: Roman Kossak, Henryk Kotlarski, Anna Engelking, and Witold Krajewski.

Thanks also go to those who helped promote this book among the Polish-speaking audiences in the West, in particular to: Teresa and

Jerzy Barankiewicz, Margaret Berczyński, François Brousseau, Ewa and Tomasz Dżurak, Victor Goliat, Ilona Gruda, Ed Harley, Ewa Hauser, Michael Hochman, Małgorzata and Krzysztof Matyjaszewski, Antony Polonsky, Adam Ringer, Leon Rozenbaum, Eugenia Shrut, Viola Wein, Lily Wysiński, and Gwido Zlatkes. Special thanks go to Andrzej Rabczenko who carried many copies of my book from Poland to America literally "on his back."

I wish to thank Mary Hrabowska, whose New York City home was a place of work and a friendly haven away from home for more than six months. For their warm hospitality, I also wish to thank Elizabeth Belk, James H. Archbold, Manuela Dobos, Sławka Kosińska, Olga Lakszin and Borys Gołowin, Ella and Peter Lewin, Paola Olecka, Shelly and Robert Pearlman, Ewa Pytowska, Żanetta Miluk, Vera Rozenbaum, Piotr Szafrański, Halina Szejnwald Brown, Zofia Siejka, Dana and Wilbur Schwartz, Róża Szatkowska, Helena and Jerzy Wrzos, and Margalit Zabludowski.

For their assistance with various organizational matters, I wish to express my gratitude to Rabbi Chaskiel Besser, Alexander Buchsbajew, the late Lucjan Dobroszycki, Kajetan Kwiatkowski, Irena Lasota, Victor Melman, the late Albin Schiff, Marek Web, and Andrzej Zabłudowski.

My profound thanks go to the Kosciuszko Foundation for making my trip to the United States possible and for facilitating my stay in the country. For its part in supporting my stay, I am grateful to the Alexander Hertz Foundation, ArtsLink, the Foundation for Jewish Philanthropies in Buffalo, New York, and the YIVO Institute for Jewish Research in New York City.

I also wish to express again my gratitude to the Polish Ministry of Culture and National Heritage, the Culture Foundation, as well as Krystyna Bratkowska, Ewa Nawrocka, Andrzej Rusak, Stefan Starczewski, and Piotr Stomma for making the appearance of the Polish edition possible.

I feel profoundly privileged to have made the acquaintance of and befriended many wonderful individuals—too many to list here—who have inspired and encouraged me during the writing of this book. I thank them all profusely.

Index of People

About the Author

Joanna Wiszniewicz is a writer and researcher at the Jewish Historical Institute in Warsaw, Poland.

✿

Jewish Lives

For a complete list of titles, see the Northwestern University Web site at www.nupress.northwestern.edu.

THOMAS TOIVI BLATT
From the Ashes of Sobibor: A Story of Survival

IDA FINK
A Scrap of Time and Other Stories

LALA FISHMAN AND STEVEN WEINGARTNER
Lala's Story: A Memoir of the Holocaust

LISA FITTKO
Escape through the Pyrenees
Solidarity and Treason: Resistance and Exile, 1933–1940

HANS FRANKENTHAL
The Unwelcome One: Returning Home from Auschwitz

RICHARD GLAZAR
Trap with a Green Fence: Survival in Treblinka

HENRYK GRYNBERG
Children of Zion
The Jewish War *and* The Victory

INGEBORG HECHT
Invisible Walls *and* To Remember Is to Heal

JOST HERMAND
A Hitler Youth in Poland: The Nazi's Program for Evacuating Children during World War II

GERTRUD KOLMAR
My Gaze Is Turned Inward: Letters, 1934–1943